To Susan  David,

I hope that you enjoy

this book. You will

always have a special

place in our heart.

Ziad

Rocambole

How we found simplicity in the
Vermont Northeast Kingdom

Ziad H. Moukheiber

To Henry, Leslie and James

with love

Table of Contents

Rocambole

Introduction

The present is a moment squeezed between the past and the future – and few people seem to enjoy it. We plan, we rush, we schedule, we are busy, and we often wonder, "Is this life?"

We plan for retirement and for college education. We pick up and drop off. To make sure we don't miss events we take pictures and movies, and we live our lives through a lens that is getting smaller and smaller. Fathers work and travel; mothers either work or worry because they are not working. Technology fuels the frenzy and makes us feel as if we are always behind schedule and too late for life's important events. We rush through life running after a perceived goal that, when we reach it, does not seem to exist. Breakfast, lunch, and dinner have been taken over by packaged food or take-out. Family life seems like a distant memory of childhood. We treat behavioral issues with electronic devices and we try to fix divorces in musty and smelly therapist offices. We experience nature through TV documentaries because the simple fern growing in our backyard is not interesting enough; we need to see a great white shark attacking a seal, or the exotic fish that live deep in the Marianas Trench. We eat and cook products that are so far removed from their origins that our children think that chickens are square.

Everything we do is by design, not by choice. Do I love my job, or am I doing it because it fits on my résumé? How does it help our kids get into schools that will take them on field trips to see a cow being milked? We build huge houses and don't even live in them. We construct islands in kitchens that we are supposed to gather around. Considering the vast numbers of kitchen islands, SUVs, large-screen TVs, sports events, and other human conveniences, we should all be very happy all the time, but shrinks and therapists and marriage counselors are prospering – not to mention divorce lawyers.

I once heard that when dealing with a situation that you don't like or have doubts about, a good exercise is to turn it upside down and investigate the exact opposite. What could be the opposite of our hectic and stressful life? Is there a simple equation to produce an effect of sanity and connection to the elements of nature? Is there a place where no one is in a rush and where all your senses are in tune with life? Where your therapist is nature itself; where the marriage counselor is an occasional rabbit, deer, or bear coming to visit; where one can sit and spend time with family with no interruptions and live simply?

For each person, there is a place like that. As Voltaire said, "We must cultivate our own garden." Your own garden may be in your imagination; it may be a physical place. For our family it became a small corner of the Northeast Kingdom.

The House

Journey of Discovery

On Mother's Day in 2008 my wife Lamia and I woke up early and told our children that we were going on a day trip to Vermont. Henry, Leslie, and James are good travelers and don't complain much, especially when promised breakfast on the road.

I had spent the previous three years scouting the East Coast for a property that would bring us closer to nature. I was not sure what I was looking for but I made it a habit to follow my instincts. Our Garden of Eden had to be a good-size piece of land not too close, not too far, not too expensive, and away from the usual destinations for urban weekenders.

Having grown up in Lebanon, a tiny country barely the size of Rhode Island, owning land is a visceral need and I had to find that special place that my family could enjoy for years to come. Purchasing real estate, as opposed to the transient passage through a hotel or inn, represents a commitment to the community. The next best thing to buying real estate is renting a house, which is another way to experience a place as if we were permanent residents. For five years we had rented a house in Bonnieux, Provence and had found a village where people were still authentic. We wanted to capture that feeling in the United States.

We loved our home in Boston. We still do. But something was missing. We felt disconnected from the rhythms of nature and the cycles of life. Our kids didn't know where their food came from before it appeared in the package at the supermarket. We missed the smell of soil and the wildness of woodland creatures that don't depend upon human owners to feed them.

As my research progressed I heard about the Northeast Kingdom. I did not really understand much about this area so I started calling real estate agents and asking them to explain. None really did, as if they were trying to protect it from people who don't need to come. The intrigue kept growing and I finally found a nice lady by the name of Sue Dukette who was willing to talk and show us some properties. I told Sue that I was looking for a minimum of fifty acres. I was guessing; I had no idea how much was fifty acres. I later discovered that fifty acres is a lot of land.

The more I learned, the more excited I became. The Northeast Kingdom is in the northeast corner of the state of Vermont, comprising Essex, Orleans, and Caledonia Counties. Roughly eighty percent of the Northeast Kingdom is covered by forest, and the area has been listed in the North American and international editions of *1,000 Places to See Before You Die,* the *New York Times* best-selling book by

Patricia Schultz. The National Geographic Society has named the Northeast Kingdom as the most desirable place to visit in the country and the ninth most desirable place to visit in the world. Roaming wild throughout the forests and fields are moose, black bear, deer, bobcats, coyotes, badgers, foxes, and fisher cats. In the pastures and skies you'll see falcons, loons, wild turkeys, and quail.

So on a muddy, cloudy day, with Lamia at the wheel of the family Volvo (I am legally blind, and therefore my dear wife must do all the driving), we drove north to Vermont. Lamia was being a good sport because she was very skeptical of my plans, she did not want to visit during the dreaded mud season, and she was worried that we'd get sucked into a financial endeavor that we would later regret.

Little did we know that we were embarking on an adventure that would transform our lives.

Once we had driven through New Hampshire, where we go skiing every winter, we entered unfamiliar territory. We drove past Franconia

Notch and the sky cleared up. The kids – no doubt remembering the day we were investigating Prince Edward Island for a real estate adventure and they were in the car for seven hours – started demanding, "Mom and Dad, where are we *going*?"

The meeting with Sue was in Irasburg, a small town of about a thousand souls located near Lake Mephremagog, about fifteen miles south of the Canadian border. Sue was a very nice lady, wearing a blue rain jacket and speaking slowly with a hint of a French Canadian accent. She asked us to follow her car, which we did, through the rolling hills along Route 14. I totally lost track of direction and had no idea where we were. Thankfully Lamia seemed to know roughly where we were.

Our first stop was at a typical Vermont farmhouse on the side of the road with a small bit of land in front. The house consisted of a series of small rooms and the wood floors cracked as we walked through. My disappointment may have shown, as I had imagined spacious open floor plans, exposed wood, views down a long driveway, and cows grazing in a field – all those things that city folk like me imagine a farmhouse to be. I came quickly to understand what a true farmhouse really means. In this part of Vermont there are only about four frost-free months during the year, and the rooms were small because years ago people had to heat their houses with wood. The houses were built close to the road so they could get wood and other necessities to the house without having to carry them long distances. Windows were small so heat loss would be minimized.

Sue then took us to another house, newer than the first. It was right along the Black River and had some land in the back, with a small pond and a root cellar. I didn't have strong feelings about it, other than to think that we didn't come all the way to Vermont to stay in a house that looked the same as the one we had in Boston.

The third place we visited was also an old charming farmhouse, but all the rooms were very small and the road separating the house from the land was not so good for the kids. The kids loved the owners who spoke some French.

We Meet the Edgertons

The last house on the list, which, based on my assessment of the photos I had seen online I had initially suggested we skip, was about ten miles south of Irasburg, in the little town of Craftsbury. The listing sheet said that it had been built in 1865. Lamia insisted we take a look but we both had low expectations and thought that while it was a nice idea to visit, it would not be a good fit for us.

Along the way many of the houses had junk in their yards: old cars, tractors, toys, farm implements, furniture, barrels – you name it. This was authentic rural Vermont, certainly not the picture perfect and gentrified towns of southern Vermont. I was accustomed to junk in the yards because in the mountain villages of Lebanon where I grew up, people store all kinds of stuff in their gardens and yards.

We followed Sue along Route 14, made a right on Wild Branch Road, and then another right on Paquette. We went along the dirt road up a hill and then parked in front of a small, typical New England farmhouse. I was starting to get tired, and the exterior of the house with its overgrown bushes did not make much of an impression on me. We parked on the short driveway. To our right was a shed with a tractor parked at the far end bay.

As we got out of the car we were greeted by Elizabeth and Phillip Edgerton, their real estate agent, and friend named Betsy. The kids were under special instructions to be on their best behavior, and we entered the house through the mudroom, which looked attractive with wood paneling on the walls. We came straight into the kitchen, which was tidy, with a bowl of bananas on the middle island and a vase of freshly cut daffodils on the breakfast table. Straight across was the brick chimney with the wood stove on the other side of it. As we passed through to the dining room we noticed that the ceilings were higher than we expected, and the living room with its grand piano featured a spacious cathedral ceiling and French doors leading to a small fieldstone terrace.

We walked upstairs to the mezzanine where there were two bedrooms and one bathroom. The old hardwood floorboards were very wide.

The basement was a bit of a shock because it was built with the original large foundation stones. The Edgertons then took us across the yard to another structure that they called the cottage – a small house with two rooms on the ground floor and a loft upstairs.

After our tour we thanked our hosts and returned to the car to start our journey home. I was tired and disappointed and did not think that any of the houses – including the last one – were a good fit. Perhaps I don't really know how to choose a house.

I dutifully asked Lamia for her thoughts about the Edgerton's house, and to my great surprise she exclaimed, "I love it!"

"Are you serious?" I said.

She had seen the potential of the place.

We came back to Boston with the feeling that one has when he or she meets a person that they know they will one day marry but can't really understand why or how it happened.

I emailed Sue, telling her that we were interested in the Craftsbury house and would like to talk about price and also go back for another visit. One would think that we would proceed cautiously and talk to someone about our plans, ask questions about the town, compare houses, and talk to neighbors. But that wasn't our style. We zeroed in on this house and assumed that everything else would fall into place.

Two weeks later we went back to Craftsbury. It was a four-hour drive from our home in Boston but we felt as though we were in a different world. We spent more time in the house and with Elizabeth and Phillip, and found them to be extremely nice. I must confess that I was clueless about farmhouses, farming, Vermont, and any related topic. So everything they talked about was fascinating to me and I tried not to ask stupid questions. We learned that the property included one hundred acres of woods behind the house, but because it was raining during both of our visits we did not make a foray into the acreage. I have to confess that I was scared to go into the woods – they seemed dark and mysterious and full of unknown creatures.

The Shoe

During this second visit Phillip Edgerton, who spoke in a deep voice filled with kindness, asked me to come with him. With great excitement and care he showed me two items. One was a photo of one of his children ski racing, because he had heard that our kids raced. The other was a nineteenth-century child's leather shoe. The shoe had been discovered in one of the walls of the house. It had been kept and passed from owner to owner. It was an old tradition to hide a kid's shoe in the wall for good luck – a tradition which we are now happy to honor.

In Lebanon a lot of people, especially taxi drivers in the 1980s, used to have a baby shoe hanging from their mirror for good luck. Those guys needed all the luck they could get because a war was raging in the country.

We Buy the House

On Friday, June 2, we made an offer. When Lamia and I signed and sent the letter to Sue we looked at each other, wondering what were we getting into. We each secretly hoped that they would refuse our offer and let this whole affair fade away. That night, Lamia, who is usually a deep sleeper, couldn't sleep. Consumed by a rising sense of panic, she kept waking me up. There was little that I could do except encourage her to relax and have faith that whatever would happen was meant to happen.

On Monday Sue called and told me that Elizabeth and Phillip had accepted our offer. We were stunned, worried, happy, excited, and anxious.

We did not get cold feet, but forged ahead with further discussions. The inspector had pointed out that the original stone foundation was caving in and needed to be replaced. The Edgertons agreed to adjust the purchase price accordingly, and we went about getting quotes from builders. Lamia and I agreed that we would not tell a soul about our crazy plan until the closing. Perhaps we were afraid that someone might try to dissuade us.

On June 28 in Stowe, Vermont we met the Edgertons and their lawyer to sign the closing. Prior to closing we had met them in the house for a last check and the house was impeccable and empty. Once the deal was signed and we all emerged into daylight and the picturesque town of Stowe, we noticed that Elizabeth and Phil went into a nearby church. I told Lamia that they were some of the nicest people I had ever met and that I believed in karma and it made me really happy to buy their house that they had owned for ten years. The closing was at noon and that same afternoon we had four beds and a new refrigerator delivered to the house.

Along with Java, our dog, we spent the first night in the old Vermont house that we later named Rocambole Farm, in honor of the variety of garlic with the distinctive looped stalk.

The next morning, the house devoid of any groceries, Lamia drove a half-hour to Morrisville, which is the largest nearby town, to get breakfast. At the time we did not know that Craftsbury has two village stores that serve excellent breakfasts. Live and learn.

Hop 66

On the day of the closing Elizabeth Edgerton gave the kids a large blue bouncing ball with two handles sticking out of the top. The kids could sit on it, hold the handle, and bounce. The ball was very sturdy and probably built prior to the made-in-China days. Emblazoned on the side of the blue ball were the enigmatic words "Hop 66." The ball became part of the scenery and almost like a pet. It gained a personality of its own, just like the volleyball in the movie *Cast Away*. We'd run around the house saying, where is Hop 66? Can you please move Hop 66 so we can drive out of the driveway? Hop 66 was everywhere and nowhere – it would disappear for a few days and then magically reappear. Hop 66 was sat on, bounced on, kicked, used as a weapon for fighting, and many more uses. And it was always left but never put away.

First Things First: The Foundation

We had scheduled a meeting with Chris Nichols, a builder from Stowe who had been recommended to us by the lawyer who did the closing. We needed to discuss rebuilding the foundation of the house, which was no easy project – it required jacking up the house, removing the stones, and pouring a concrete foundation. Right on time, Chris parked his black pickup truck in the driveway. I was impressed by his appearance – he was wearing really cool sunglasses, jeans, and a white t-shirt, and he looked like a rugged New England builder with rough hands and a face battered by the weather, long hours of construction work, and too many cigarettes.

We sat on the terrace table that we had brought inside so we could sit together and have meals with the kids. We gave Chris a tour of the house and sat back down to ask him if he could do it. He said, "Yep."

That is when the situation hit me. We had just

bought a farmhouse in an area we did not know and now we were giving our newly acquired property to a man we had met only once, who was going to come back and dig up our precious home with an eleven-ton excavator.

I asked Chris if he would mind coming back the next day because I wanted to see him twice before writing him a fat check and giving him the keys to the house. I also asked him for a contract or some kind of an agreement. He looked me in the eye and said that a handshake was as good as a contract.

The next morning he returned, and – I suppose solely to please me – he presented a contract written in pencil on a yellow legal pad. I thought I would just as well go with the handshake. So we gave him a big check and prayed that we were not making a huge mistake.

Chris said that he would start the work the next day, Monday. We returned to Boston and spent a stressful week wondering if this adventure were real. Did we really buy a farm in Vermont and did we really just pay a random man to destroy it?

The following Friday we drove up with the plan to sleep in the cottage and see whether Chris had started the work. The cottage did not have any furniture, so I had called the same mattress store and ordered more mattresses. The salesperson laughed because the previous week I had bought four. I insisted that four more had to be delivered on Friday; otherwise, we had no place to sleep.

When we got to the house, with a mixture of delight and horror we found the house surrounded by an eight-foot-deep trench, the terrace completely gone, and mud everywhere.

For the following two months Chris battled mud and rain like they had never seen in the area for decades. He dug up the foundation, removed all the stones, and poured a new concrete foundation. In the process he leveled the house, with the unintended consequence that the doors, which had all been perfectly fitted for an unleveled house, wouldn't close properly.

We watched his work carefully and he did quite an impressive job without even scratching the outside of the house. The chimney had to be reinforced because we asked Chris to dig a bit deeper to create more headroom in the basement.

During this process new words including curtain drain, septic system, and leach field became too familiar to us.

In order to excavate the basement, Chris had to tear up the heating system, which meant that before winter set in we needed to find a plumber to install a new heating system. He had also removed the small porch in front of the main door and took out the terrace, which was very small to begin with. It dawned on us that the rebuilding of the foundation was just one piece of the plan, and we had not thought ahead to figure out the ramifications.

Sheep's Milk Cheese

Phillip Edgerton had mentioned the name of the builder who built the cottage – Harry Miller. I was starting to get confused about the word "builder." Who is a builder? Everyone in Vermont seemed to be a builder! Anyway, I called Harry and told him we were the new owners of the Edgerton's house and that we would love to meet him. We made an appointment to meet the first weekend in August.

On the appointed day Harry parked his black pickup truck in our driveway. We greeted him and showed him around. He looked as if he knew the house really well, which he did – as a teenager he and his buddies used to come and party in the house, which was abandoned at the time. Years later he built the cottage, the dormers on the second floor, and the kitchen island. He was extremely friendly, but had the interesting habit of twisting his neck in a sign of questioning or worrying about what was being done to the house. I think that he was a bit puzzled as to who was this guy with the Lebanese accent and what was he doing in Vermont in the Edgerton's place. I didn't mind; I later learned that Harry loved and respected Elizabeth and Phillip, and I'm sure he felt some sadness that they had sold the place.

For someone who was supposed to be a reticent Vermonter, he asked me a lot of questions and he kept looking me straight in the eye. Finally, out of the blue, he said, "You seem like a good man." This was reassuring.

We agreed to meet again the following week and to draw up a list of items we needed help with, including the heat. To nearly every issue I raised, Harry only said, "No problem – don't worry about it."

He asked me what we were planning to do in Vermont. I told him that we would like to farm and also one day to make cheese. He asked what our favorite cheese was. I said, "It's a French cheese called *fromage de brebis,* which is sheep's milk cheese – but I'm sure you don't have any here."

Harry left and we took the kids to Morrisville to raid the hardware store – we needed *everything*. We came back at around three in the afternoon and found at our doorstep a small package with Harry's business card upon which he had written, "Welcome to Vermont." Inside the package was a slice of delicious sheep's milk cheese from Bonnieview Farm. It was delicious!

That's when we knew we had found the right place.

Summer of Mud

Throughout the summer the house was a full construction site with no less than two big excavators and a Bobcat onsite every day. One day Chris came to me and said, "I have some bad news. The septic tank is leaking and you need a new one." Since I was not about to personally inspect the septic tank leak, I agreed to buy a new one. The following week a truck came and dropped the new tank in the mud. I did not think that we would ever not have mud around the house and I should start getting used to it.

The following week Chris came to me and said, "I have bad news and good news. The well pump got hit by lightning. The good news is that it's under warranty and the company is going to replace it." From this conversation I learned that we have a well on the property, and that wells have pumps in them.

By the end of August, Chris had created a concrete basement, a bunch of curtain drains, and a swale that went around the back of the house for drainage. He built a little bridge over the swale with a pipe going under the bridge. Finally he seeded the topsoil he had spread, and covered it with hay using a hay cannon on his truck. On August 29 Chris shook my hand and said, "Once in a while a builder meets a client like you, and I thank you for the business." Sadly, our project was his last job before the economy crashed. He was hard hit and eventually had to find other work.

The Mailbox

Since buying the house we had not gotten any mail. Lamia had to drive to the Post Office in Craftsbury to get it, and we did not know why we had to do this. Finally the lady at the Post Office told us that our mailbox was not installed to official specifications, and she gave Lamia a sheet with instructions. An approved mailbox had to be exactly forty-four inches high and not too far from the edge of the road and not shaky.

We bought a new mailbox pole and asked Chris to dig a hole with his excavator. We set up the new mailbox post and attached the mailbox. We had been advised to use the same funky old mailbox in order to avoid mailbox-bashing, a local tradition in which young people drive by and smash your mailbox. They particularly love to bash shiny new ones.

So the following day the mailbox was ready, and we were eager to see the mail lady deliver us some mail. As we watched with breathless anticipation her car stopped at the box and then drove away. We hurried to the box and opened it and found no mail – only a yellow sheet with the government mailbox regulations. Next to "height" was a crisp check mark. I dutifully measured the box and discovered that our box was *one inch* too low. We yanked up the post, stuck a rock in the hole, and the next day we were delighted to open our mailbox to find our mail.

Harry Gets to Work

As September dawned, Lamia and I looked at each other and said, "Now what?" We had no terrace, no landscaping, no heat, and no porch. But now it was Harry Miller's turn to go to work.

Harry struck me as a very good man who builds his relationships on honesty and integrity. He took on the "patient" and started performing a long list of operations that would last for a year. His first job was to help install a big underground propane tank and run the line to the back of the kitchen. I spent an afternoon in the trench with him, talking more than helping, but getting to know him. He advised us to put a layer of a kind of plaster over the outside insulation so it would not rot.

Next came the laundry room. The washer and drier were in the kitchen with the drier venting to the inside of the kitchen, following the suggestion of the architect of the cottage, who had recommended that in winter this helps to keep moisture in the house. We didn't see it this way, and to us a big problem was the fabric dust that the drier spewed out into the kitchen.

There was a solution. When you entered the house through the mudroom, the first door on the left opened into a windowless room where there was a two-person Jacuzzi. The walls were covered with Caribbean island view wallpaper and the room had a moldy, musky smell that made your head spin. We decided the new room would become the laundry room. Harry ripped out the Jacuzzi and with a surgeon's precision installed a window that, as an unexpected bonus, made the façade of the house symmetrical. In the process he discovered that the overhang was a trap for mice, and dozens of mice had fallen in the hole, could not get out, and had died in the heat.

These first two jobs showed that Harry was honest, reliable, and a perfectionist, so we opened the floodgates of projects. We gave Harry the go-ahead to do all of the "we-might-as-well-do-it" projects: changing all the doorknobs, repainting the interior, finishing the basement, putting a door on the garage, and redoing all the floors.

In the cottage Harry installed a rope railing on the ladder that went up to the loft. I had found a length of boat-docking rope of three inches in diameter and Harry installed two poles and drilled holes in them and passed the rope through. It looked really nice and fit very well in the style of the cottage.

Harry and his colleague Sean, who is a fireman, worked on the house and spent most of the winter doing all the interior work from painting to drywall to tiling the new basement bathroom. We did not use an architect for the basement; we just stood there while Harry outlined the different rooms by placing two-by-fours on the ground. In Vermont, everything is influenced by the seasons, and they both wanted to finish the job before the spring and summer, which are their busy outdoor building seasons. Sean is a volunteer fireman in Craftsbury and we met him first at the Craftsbury Firemen's annual chicken barbeque.

During Thanksgiving week we were at the house and asked Harry if we could do anything to help. He suggested we help him treat the pine boards he bought for all the doors and trim. We had to paint them with a product called WATCO, one of our first encounters with a toxic substance used in Vermont.

As we were working to paint all the pine boards with WATCO, our children started getting fidgety and were underfoot more than they were helpful. We decided to "get rid of them" and suggested that they pack a backpack with snacks, compass, a knife, ropes, etc., and go exploring in the woods. We gave them a walkie-talkie and kept the other by our side. Having pushed them in the direction of the trail, we got back to more productive work. We were working so well that we completely forgot about the kids until Lamia looked at her watch and realized that an hour had gone by. She radioed the kids to make sure they were all right. Henry answered and said in a breathless voice: "We just saw a bear and we are coming home!"

Never have three children run home so fast or been so happy to see their parents. To this day we are not sure whether what they saw was a bear, a fisher cat, or a very suspicious-looking tree, but to them it was real, it was scary, and, most importantly, it was an adventure.

My then-six-year-old son James took to the building profession as though it were designed especially for him. When he heard that we were to help out Sean and Harry, he took his "job" very seriously and asked Sean if he could work with him. Sean, who himself has a two-year-old son, kindly said yes.

One morning James, who normally has to be coaxed out of bed and into street clothes, appeared at our bedside promptly at 7:00 am and announced that he was leaving for work. Lamia opened a sleepy eye and, unable to believe that her child had miraculously been able to get out of bed, pick out his clothes, and get dressed without any nagging, asked, "What job?"

"I'm working with Sean today to help tile the

bathroom," answered James, and he promptly left the cottage for the main house and his new job. As Sean – and James – were busy at work tiling the new bathroom, Sean's walkie-talkie suddenly crackled to life and announced that a fire had broken out in a house on Wild Branch Road. Sean washed his hands and rushed to the scene. Now he is viewed as a household hero, rushing from his day job to save people. James could not have been more proud of "his colleague."

The Bird

One morning a few months after we had bought the house I woke up early as usual and did my regular walk around the house. I loved going around early in the morning to check on things. As time went by I mustered more courage and started walking in a larger loop into the forest and into fields. I took the turn around the garage and passed one of the old apple trees. At the base of the tree was a large, dead bird (a grouse, I later learned). The bird was leaning on the tree. It baffled me as to how this bird got there. It was leaning against the tree as if it just walked to the tree and leaned against it and died. I looked up the tree for any clue and I thought that maybe the bird had a heart attack and fell down but it was leaning against the tree. The fact that it was leaning against the tree made a lot of scenarios not possible.

We had heard on the news about the West Nile virus and the number of birds that were found dead as a result of the disease. Upon further inspection of the fowl, I was convinced that this bird had been sick and walked up to the base of the tree, exhausted, and just leaned back and died. I ran inside and frantically told everyone to stay away from the dead bird – it had to be diseased and full of infection and contagions.

I found two sticks and a piece of cardboard. Without touching the bird I pushed it on the cardboard with the sticks and carried it to the small fire pit we had made. The pit still had some wood in it so I placed the cardboard and the bird on top of the wood and placed the two sticks that had touched the bird on top as well (to avoid spreading the virus, the tools had to be destroyed). I then poured gasoline on top of it and lit the whole thing. It burst into flames almost in an explosive way and I watched as the bird was incinerated along with the wood and any diseases. I went in for breakfast, feeling good that I had stopped this potentially dangerous spread of a virus.

An hour later Harry pulled up in the driveway to drop off some wood. "Did you show the bird to the kids?" he said. "I left it for you at the base of the tree." He said that often times when trying to take off, birds fly into the windows of houses and break their necks.

I felt very stupid and started laughing but did not tell him why. I will not be viewed as the ignorant city man. After that event I would often spot grouse birds and hear them in the woods. The sound of their wings is almost like a helicopter trying to take off.

The Transition House

Right across the driveway from the house is a Shaker shed that Harry had built. It was really useful because one can work on a rainy day or even run in for shelter if a thunderstorm suddenly erupts. Inside the shed I found a sign on a short pole that said "Transition." I did not know why there was a sign that said Transition. Maybe there was a race of some sort – a triathlon – and this marked the transition where people switched from bikes to running.

Somehow I knew that this was as farfetched as my bird-leaning-against-the-tree story.

I had forgotten about the sign until one day Harry was talking about the cottage that he had built and mentioned that it was used as a transition house. The Edgertons made the cottage available to anyone in their community needing a place to stay until they got back on their feet. This was very touching and added more assets to our karma bank.

Robbie, and Vermont's Heating and Hunting Season

With fall approaching, we insisted that the priority was the heat, and Harry kept reassuring me that it was no problem to get it done by November. He gave me the number of a plumber named Robbie. I called Robbie and left my number with his wife or girlfriend, and never got a call back. I am sure with my Arabic name there may have been some confusion about my purpose for the call. I called Harry again and told him that he needed to call Robbie, which he did.

Robbie was a really nice guy and he seemed to have a good sense of humor, but I did not get to spend much time with him. One of the things that I learned about him was that he was an avid hunter. Every religion has its high holy holidays, and in Vermont, it's the winter hunting season. Depending on the furry or feathered animal you want to shoot with a gun, hunt with a bow and arrow, and/or catch in a trap, the season lasts from September until March. I knew that if Robbie didn't get the job done before he headed off to the fields, we would freeze until the spring thaw.

With two floors of radiant heat (basement and ground level) and regular radiators upstairs, the project was not a simple one. In late September, Robbie started the work and turned a small utility room into heat-and-hot-water headquarters, with pipes and pumps going everywhere in neat rows and in pretty copper colors. It was a pleasure to see the end result of his work. By the time Robbie needed to go off to do his hunting, he had the basement and the ground floor systems installed. Good enough, according to Harry, to keep the house warm until the end of November.

The house was surrounded by woods, and soon these woods were full of people using all manner of weaponry. Assuming you have the correct hunting license, beginning in September you can hunt black bear. Then comes shotgun and bow-and-arrow turkey season, and then Youth

Deer Weekend. Then it's deer rifle season, deer muzzleloader season (just like Davey Crockett), and deer bow-and-arrow season. You can also hunt or trap raccoon, red and gray foxes, otter, muskrat, beaver, bobcat, fisher cats, gray squirrel, ruffed grouse, hare, rabbit, woodcock, and migratory waterfowl. Basically, if it has four legs or feathers, at some point during the fall or winter you can kill it and mount it on your wall or, more importantly, stock your freezer for the winter.

I did not want a good citizen of Vermont to inadvertently shoot at our house. Because rifle bullets can travel a long way (as opposed to shotgun pellets), I first had to set up a perimeter around the house with safety signs that alerted hunters that a house was in the vicinity. Then we had to get equipped with bright orange attire when walking outside, while avoiding looking like tourists worried about getting shot in our own backyard. The dog also got an orange jacket.

I did not like the "trollers." Basically, trollers

are guys who load their trucks with beer and drive around looking for deer to shoot at. To say the least, they do not inspire much confidence.

Prior to the hunting season you hear a lot of gunshots in the woods; these are folks practicing. During the season you hear the occasional shot and then the news travels fast of someone shooting a multi-point deer, which is the number of points on their antlers – the more, the better. If you do shoot a deer, you probably eviscerate it on site, and then load it on the back of your pickup. You leave the back open and slowly drive around the neighborhood just to make sure that everybody gets a good look at your kill.

Some game is scarce, and the number of permits is highly restricted. Vermont holds two annual lotteries – one for moose permits, and one for "antlerless" permits. Each year the number of permits offered in the lottery varies, depending on the biological conditions of the herds. The lucky hunters are those who win the lottery and get the opportunity to hunt a moose.

The hunting fever got to me and I learned about bow hunting equipment. Once I knew what I wanted, I searched Craigslist and found a seventy-pound-draw compound bow. In plain English, this means that pulling back on the string is very difficult for a regular city person. When guests visit the house, they often want to try the bow but they can't pull the string back. Thankfully, at that time I was working out in preparation for a biking race up Mount Washington, so I managed to draw the bow. I tried it behind the house and with the first two shots I badly scraped my forearm. My respect for hunting grew when I imagined myself hanging twenty feet off the ground in a tree with multiple layers of clothing to avoid freezing and pulling the bow without the deer hearing me.

Much to our relief, by the tenth of December Robbie was back from hunting and got the heating system fully installed and ready for the winter season. He had gotten lucky in the moose-hunting lottery and had shot a moose with a bow. He left in our freezer six pounds of moose meat in a variety of different cuts. The meat was delicious cooked with garlic and herbs.

Eugene the Electrician

Meanwhile, Harry worked on the rest of the projects and did his fair share of hunting, too. I knew that because he does not use his cell phone (not that there is much reception anyway), so the only window of opportunity to talk to him during hunting season was for one hour each day, from 7:30 pm to 8:30 pm. Most of the time when I called I spoke with Harry's wife Jean. She is a lovely woman, who has patiently fielded numerous calls from me in pursuit of the elusive Harry.

One day, Eugene, the electrician, showed up with his son – both dressed in camouflage – to take a look at the house and the cottage to see what needed to be done. We asked Eugene to change all the old yellowy electric switches and plugs to a new model that was clean and contemporary; we were going for a modern farmhouse look. I had no idea how many electrical plugs and switches a house had.

We gave Eugene his list, and we soon got used to

the idea that everyone would come and do their work whenever they chose. The key was hidden outside and every weekend when we arrived from Boston we enjoyed trying to discover what progress had been made. Some days we would come and little had been done, and other days – to our delight – major progress had been made.

Together with Chris, Harry, and Robbie, Eugene was now officially part of the house. We understood that the house was not really ours – a lot of local residents claimed memories and stories of the house and the people who had lived in it. We knew that some day, our time in the house would become part of that same rich heritage. Being raised in Lebanon, where so many buildings are not only old but are ancient, I embraced this as the way things naturally are and should be. We are not owners, but stewards. During the process of remodeling the house we always tried to respect the integrity of the house and honor the traditions of the land.

Smile – You're on Candid Camera

One weekend in February we came to check on things and I walked in snow over my knees to the cottage. I found the cottage a bit cold, even though it is a well-insulated structure. That day the temperature had gone down to zero degrees Fahrenheit, but I did not make much of it until the next morning, when I found that the pipes in the cottage had frozen. I called Harry immediately and we rushed in a plumber from Morrisville. We bought two electric heaters and ran the fireplace full strength. This was a close call and I realized that during our absences we had no way of verifying that the heat was on.

I found that a local company, Bourne's Energy of Morrisville, offered a service called Home Heat Monitoring, and that if they got a signal of a low temperature they would come to the house to fix the system. I rushed and signed up for the service.

While possessed by this determination to ensure against any calamity, I also set up webcams so I could monitor everything from my desk in Boston. One camera was pointing at the driveway, another at the terrace, one in the cottage, and another on the back of the house. This system allowed me to know when Harry, Eugene, and the others were in the house, or if there were any unwelcome visitors.

When the system was first installed, I watched from my office in Boston as Harry came up the driveway. I waited two minutes and called the house. Of course he was astonished, but when I told him about the camera he was thankfully not offended.

In my enthusiasm for security I added a camera inside the living room, along with a remote switch that allowed me to turn on a light from my desk in Boston. One day the camera showed only a dark blurry image. That weekend I went to the house and found that an empty potato-chip bag had been stuck in front of the camera. Harry had been having his lunch and did not want Big Brother to be watching.

The guys were good-natured about my snoopy cameras and everyone would wave and everyone thought I was watching all the time. I learned that the crew had the best work ethic I had ever seen, never missing a day and showing up and leaving at the exact same time.

The Master Plan

In the midst of all of these details, we were also considering the big picture. When Chris Nichols had ripped up the terrace and plowed and excavated everything around the house, we had begun to think about the outside of the house – the landscape, plantings, and a vision for this immense hundred-acre plot of land. Lamia had asked Chris to excavate all the existing plant material, convincing me that it was worth saving and that replacing all the plants would cost thousands of dollars. Chris had done as she had asked, gingerly ripping up large clumps of bushes and perennials and placing them temporarily in a spot that was somewhat wet to ensure their survival. At this point, Lamia and I felt that we needed a professional to help us with the planning of the land around the house, including the pond and the immediate "neighborhood" of four to five acres surrounding the house. We hadn't even explored the entire hundred-acre property –

that would come in due time.

We needed a master plan.

We contacted the architect of the cottage to see if he knew of a landscape architect. He gave us the name of Distinctive Landscaping of Charlotte, located a few miles south of Burlington. One Saturday, to accommodate our schedule, Tricia arrived at our house for a consultation, accompanied by her husband and three-year-old child. We showed her the house and property, and described our plan and vision for the place. We wanted to combine modern and old, and Mediterranean and New England, and make a place that would be a comfortable refuge from the hectic city life but that was also a working farm.

We met a few more times and went over the four-to-ten-year plan, which included a *terrain de boules*, which is a compacted sand court for the game of *boules*. Also called *pétanque,* the game is played in the south of France, where I lived for a while as a teenager. It's not unlike the Italian game of *bocce*. Each player gets two heavy metal balls (called *boules*), and to begin the game one person throws a small wooden ball (called the *cochonet*). The goal is to throw the *boules* one at a time and whoever is the closest to the *cochonet* at the end wins. The two strategies are "*tu tire ou tu pointe*" ("you shoot or you point") – one either can lob the ball and get close to the target, or shoot straight and knock the opponent's ball out of the way. The game is very social and has the Mediterranean feel that I wanted to bring to Vermont.

We also wanted a horse arena, but no swimming pool or tennis court, because we all agreed that this was a working farm. And to take advantage of the different views, I insisted on having multiple places to sit during various times of the day.

The following visit was in the spring with the owner of the firm and nursery, Charlie Proutt, coming along with Tricia. He suggested we walk around the land. Every time we walked deep in the woods we felt like we were going on a safari and needed a lot of preparation. Charlie was wearing light-colored pants and sneakers and to our astonishment strolled into the forbidding forest as calmly as he would walk into a house. What courage! Because he was full of energy and passion for the local fauna it was a pleasure to walk with him and Tricia around the acreage and learn about the various plants and trees.

The house was separated from the pond by a dirt road that came right to the door; on the other side of the road were the pond and a small field. We assumed that all the landscaping would be done on the side of the house and that we would stay away from the road and the other side. Charlie stood on the side of the pond and loved the scene and really saw the end result with Tricia, and said this should all be part of the plan.

In May Tricia came by with the master plan. They used our ideas and concepts and incorporated all the existing elements and plants to come up with a final plan that was perfect.

A large terrace would surround most of the house, with a rectangular space outside the living room flanked by two half-moon sitting areas on either side and a stone walkway all around. On the side of the kitchen, two growing areas would connect to the terrace. In front of the house would be an orchard, and across the road the *terrain de boules* and a gazebo next to the pond.

Behind the house, three long beds were planned for growing vegetables; the beds near the kitchen were for a *jardin potager*. A pergola was designed to cover the main sitting area and a short sitting wall would anchor and frame the whole thing.

The plan was simply fantastic; we only needed to figure out how to implement it piece by piece. We spent hours looking at the plan and dreaming of making it a reality.

The only work that had been done to date was a small area in front of the living room that Chris Nichols had compacted for a possible terrace. And of course, some of the choices that we had made when we first bought the house now seemed inappropriate. Lamia disliked the little bridge that Chris Nichols had built over the swale, and Charlie and Tricia agreed that it needed to be improved.

From an investment perspective I was worried that if the market crashed and we needed to sell, an unfinished property would have little value. Even if the house were finished, I was very nervous about it lacking a terrace, and building something temporary was not an option – we are not the type of people to seek temporary fixes. We have found that many times in life temporary solutions become permanent, and you are stuck with them.

Gilbert and the Purple Dragon

I called Harry and told him that we had a landscaping plan and wanted to investigate – potentially – maybe someday – implementing it, and what would he recommend? Tricia and Charlie were also looking into implementing the plan and providing us with a quote. So we coordinated a meeting between Harry, Charlie, and Gilbert, who was another member of the "Harry Team." Gilbert, whom Harry had known for years, approached excavating as if it were an art form. We all met at the house and I was consumed wanting to know what could be done. Drainage, lasers, excavation, ditches, gravel, stones – all were all discussed. Charlie gave us a quote using his crew from Burlington, but we felt strongly about using local labor.

A tall, strong man with hands of steel, Gilbert was a very nice guy with honesty written all over his face, and we knew he was as good as his handshake. We were wondering how much it would cost to do the prep work for the terrace and walkways around the house. Gilbert started working and we were still wondering – and soon we realized that the outside project was under way.

And then we met the Purple Dragon: Gilbert's excavator, a big purple 18,000-pound machine with a bucket that tilted sideways. Gilbert and the Purple Dragon started from the back to the front. Working with the precision of a surgeon, he followed Charlie's plan to the tenth of an inch, adding the stones to the sand, compacting the walkway, and creating a drip line around the house that Tricia and Charlie had not accounted for. Using my webcam in Boston, I watched as Gilbert worked, slowly and with great attention to detail. Sometimes he used a shovel and other times the Purple Dragon, but with astonishing delicacy, the way I would use a teaspoon to sprinkle sugar on strawberries. I learned that every excavator operator has a myth associated with him – that he could pick up a fallen leaf with his bucket and put it on your head, or if the teeth of the bucket were sharp he could shave you. The Purple Dragon lived at our house for a month and a half and truckloads of gravel and dirt kept coming and going. The end result was incredible – the plan we had designed was coming to life.

Anners the Stonemason

In May – now it was nearly a year after we bought the house – I kept obsessing about building the terrace. How could we possibly spend the summer on a farm in Vermont without being able to sit outside? The project went from a "project" to a "passion" to then to an "obsession." I started analyzing our options. Could we rebuild the same terrace with the same stones and implement the Tricia-and-Charlie plan during that time? But the speculation was almost irrelevant because we didn't have a stonemason. Harry mentioned that we should meet Anners and said that she builds walls. I tried to politely ignore his suggestion because I thought it was highly improbable that a woman could be a professional stonemason. But the conversation came up again and Harry once again said that we should meet Anners.

I finally agreed to meet Anners and she came on a day when the snow was still on the ground. I was in the basement talking to Harry and

Sean when Lamia called me to the dining room and said that Anners had arrived. I came up and Lamia was standing next to a young very attractive blonde woman, so I looked around the room for the stonemason. Lamia said, "Ziad, meet Anners." This was one of those tense, awkward moments where the expectation is so far from reality that you feel bad. Anners was a very calm nice young lady in her late twenties who chose as a career building stone walls, managing gardens, and planting.

So we walked around the house in the snow, and in a typical city-hectic-crazy way I described the plan and what we needed. I peppered Anners with a lot of questions – when can you start, how can you do this, what do you think of that. Anners said in a slow and calm voice, "Why don't I come back when there's no snow on the ground?" Then she looked at me and very politely told me that I needed to relax.

We had some doubts that Anners could build a stone wall or a terrace, but in the spirit of our plan we jumped right in and had faith in Harry.

We also realized that karma had been working in our favor – every local person whom we had met had been highly capable and honest, so we had every incentive to give Anners the benefit of the doubt. And so a new character joined the Rocambole pageant.

As spring melted into summer, Gilbert finished all the preparation work for Anners. In June she and her crew started with the goal to first build the terrace right in front of the living room so we could use it and the steps leading outside. Without the terrace and the steps we could not use the French doors. Gilbert had done an outstanding job outlining and compacting the areas that Anners and her team needed to build their dry stone structure. The work they did was pure stone work – no cement or mortar of any kind was used, and all the work was done by hand. We were staying true to the area by choosing the stone from a local quarry in Jeffersonville, and all the workers on Anners team were from the area.

We spent the months of June and July coming

back and forth to the house and living for long periods of time with Anners and her crew working on the terrace, and then the walkways and the half-moon terraces. As the work progressed, we realized that the stonework was another specialized aspect to the project that we had to learn about. Building a dry set terrace wall or steps is a challenge and requires strength, patience, artistic ability, and an intimate knowledge of stones. It is like building a three-dimensional puzzle with pieces that are not meant to work together by design.

For proper drainage, the floor surfaces had to have a one-percent slant to the outside. Any stagnant water around the house would freeze in the winter and would create trouble. The stone has a metallic blue tint and on a sunny day looks like a shiny blue-grey paint. The terrace stones were placed very tightly against each other, while the stones in the walkways had a bit more space between them.

The walkway and terraces were separated by perennial beds on two sides and some vegetable beds on the kitchen side. Lamia and Anners designed the beds and traveled to Cady's Falls Nursery in Morrisville to select additional plants. Lamia claims it is one of the best nurseries she has ever been to. Anners suggested we put more compost and not to use any mulch. They designed the beds to have continuously flowering plants from May to October.

One day I boasted to Anners that I could build my own wall using the dry set method, and she laughed and said that most clients say that, but never do it. I Googled "how to build a dry set wall" and watched some videos on YouTube. A dry set wall has to be as wide as it is high. It has to taper inwards about one inch per foot in height. The stones have to be set with at least three points touching, and they should overlap to be solid. The wall should have a couple of broad stones that span the width of the wall for stability. The inside section of the wall is called "fill" and could be filled with small stones. Other than the backbreaking work it was really challenging to have the patience to build it slowly.

I finally finished my small wall and showed it to Anners. She looked at it and said, "Not bad." Later, when I saw a similar project she did in Craftsbury, I saw the difference and understood that my wall was barely acceptable. The amount of patience this work required was unfathomable to a guy like me. We would sometimes leave for a week and come back to see that six or seven stones had been placed. I suppose my impatience showed because one day Anners looked at me and said, "Chill, Ziad."

The Bobcat

Anners and her team had almost finished and had a large pile of leftover stones at the front of the house that had to be moved to the terrace where Chris Nichols had left a large pile of fieldstone from the foundation. I suggested that I could help by renting a Bobcat. Anners asked me if I had ever driven one. I smiled and said, "Sure!" and of course everyone knew that I had never touched one. Undeterred, I called a large-equipment renting place and asked if they rented Bobcats. I booked one for the day when Anners and Luke, her coworker, would come and help. The day before we needed it, the rental guy dropped the Bobcat outside the house. He was about to leave when I raced outside and asked him to show me how it worked. I tried to ask in a way that showed him that I had some experience but just needed a little refresher. Like everyone else, he knew that I was clueless.

I've been skydiving, flown in small airplanes, and gone scuba diving with sharks, but operating the Bobcat was one of the most fun things I have ever done. The Bobcat is a small machine but very powerful, and as I sat in the cockpit I felt as if I were driving a flying saucer. I had two joysticks – one on each side. One drives the Bobcat forward and back, and turns. The other operates the bucket. The joysticks were fly-by-wire, just like a jet. In full throttle the Bobcat can do a 360-degree turn in one or two seconds and rip the ground while doing it. The buckets can pick up practically anything. My kids were excited to sit in my lap under the protection bar and drive it. I even let my older son Henry drive it alone while talking to me on a walkie-talkie. Because he is used to using joysticks on video games, he operated the bucket with more ease than I did.

When we were working I drove the Bobcat back and forth, moving the stones that Anners and Luke would push into the bucket. I consider myself strong, but their strength was unbelievable. Once we moved all the stones from the front of the house to the stone pile in front of the living room terrace area we were done. Anners and Luke, their long days of work at our house now completed, went on to their next job.

Me? I had four more hours to play with the Bobcat until it was scheduled to be picked up.

The master plan called for a *terrain de boules* – a court for playing *boules* – across the road. The court was going to be fifty feet long and fifteen feet wide, and I had put four stakes in the ground to outline the rectangle for future construction. The plan called for a thirty-inch-deep pit that would be filled with gravel and then sand.

My three hours in the Bobcat gave me the confidence to take on a challenging project, so without telling Lamia I decided that I was going to dig the pit for the *terrain de boules*. I drove the Bobcat to the assigned area and started digging. I only had a few hours so I kept going in and out of the pit, dumping the dirt outside. At one point I was in such a frenzy that I confused the joysticks and dumped a load of dirt on my head. The cockpit was protected by a metal roof with a grill, so while no stones fell on me a lot of dirt came through.

The other challenge I faced was that the pit had to be leveled. The field was on a small slope and that is when I realized that I had created a total mess – the pit was at it deepest five feet and was nowhere near level and looked horrible, with a large pile of dirt at the end of it. Very humbly I had to go in the house, confess what I had done, apologize to Lamia, and then call Gilbert. He brought back the Purple Dragon and beautifully fixed my mess. He even raised the end of the court to make it level.

Lamia, the kids and I later built a frame for the *terrain de boules* using pressure-treated pine. Gilbert put on the last layer of industrial sand and compacted it. The end result was perfect – it looked like an invisible-edge pool.

I Ride the Purple Dragon

When Gilbert was done he left the Purple Dragon just outside the house on the dirt where the lawn was going to be, and mentioned with a smile that the key was under the seat. At first I did not understand what he meant – and then the excitement took over. I could play with his 18,000-pound beast! I paused to think and to consider the disaster I had made using the Bobcat. I didn't think very long – the temptation was too great. But this time, I decided that to avoid risk of injury to my family, as long as I was operating the Purple Dragon everyone had to stay indoors.

I sat in the mothership cockpit and started figuring out what did what. No one had shown me anything – it was strictly trial and error. Unlike the Bobcat, this machine had only one large joystick and pedals and a bunch of knobs whose functions I did not know. This was a true challenge because you had to think in three dimensions – the arm of the excavator has two parts plus the bucket that moves forward and back and sideways. It was quite the mental challenge.

I thought of a little project that I could do with the Purple Dragon. To break the runoff of rainwater that came from the hill above and flooded the field, a small culvert crossed the road right in front of the driveway. To guide water into the culvert we had dug a small trench by shovel, but I decided to enlarge it a bit. I started digging, and at first the operation seemed simple. But I dug myself in a hole – literally – and started to panic. By the time I stopped I had excavated a five-foot-deep trench that was dangerous for the kids. Mud was everywhere and I was mentally drained. I could not figure out how to move and dig at the same time, and for the first time since I was a kid I felt ashamed – the same way a child who breaks a vase in his or her parents' living room would feel. With even more humility than I had felt during the Bobcat event, I yet again had to confess to Lamia what happened. Because paying to fix my mess could be very expensive, she was not in a forgiving mood, and I had to call Gilbert and 1) apologize for the mess, 2) beg him to fix it, 3) ask him to not charge us a lot of money, and 4) tell him that Lamia will never let me use his machine again.

I gained tremendous respect for excavator operators and the work they do.

Turning my attention to less dangerous projects, I seeded grass around the *terrain de boules* and also asked Anners to bring some stone for a small wall around the edge of the court for people to sit on. Because the field was on a slope, at the higher end the wall would be nearly flush with the ground.

The house was starting to take shape with the walkways, terraces, and the *terrain de boules* looking amazing – while nothing was grown yet, I imagined that with the blue-grey stone surrounded by the green of the grass the end result was going to be spectacular.

The remaining project was going to be a low

sitting wall of around 60 feet in length to wrap around the terrace area. We postponed this project for awhile, but when we later built the wall it showcased the terraces and perennial beds with the same effect as a frame does to a great painting.

The Pond, the Dock, and the Spring

At the beginning of July I felt that we were so involved with the house and farm that we needed to pay a bit more attention to the kids; they were no longer doing their usual activities in Boston which included swimming and playing tennis. We needed a solution for swimming, and across the road near the new *terrain de boules* there was the pond.

We tried swimming in the pond, but walking through the muck on the edge was a deterrent and the kids, city folks by birth, refused to stick a little toe in the muck. A solution had to be found.

A swimming pool was too expensive and really not a good fit on a working farm. After spending a good amount of time online figuring out what to do, I found a company in the area that sold floating docks that were designed specifically for use in ponds with marshy borders. I placed the order and asked them to rush it, and a few days later a large flatbed truck arrived and the driver dropped the dock next to the pond. The dock was extremely heavy but we managed to drag it to the spot we had chosen and push it into the water. Then we installed the cedar panels and planted the two pipes that hold it in place at the edge of the pond.

The dock was in the shape of a "T" and so it was very stable. This created in an instant a swimming area that could be used all summer long by the kids and their friends. We allowed our kids to swim and we blithely assured everyone else that the pond was always full of nice clean water.

Not quite. There wasn't much rain that summer and the level of the pond started dropping. We may also have been the cause of a change in the underground water; to ensure a dry area for the *terrain de boules* we had built a curtain drain right over the court.

The pond water level declined so low that we could not longer swim. Something needed to be done, but I did not know how to bring water to the pond without spending huge amounts of money.

A chance conversation provided the key. Our farm is on Paquette Road, which is the family name of our two neighbors below us. Driving down the road, on the right live Mark and Penny, and on the left is Mark's father Wilfred, aged 87. Wilfred has lived all of his life on Paquette Road and he had taken daily walks up and down the road. Because of his advancing years he couldn't walk very far, so every day around 5:00 pm he would drive his car up the road and back. I made it habit to try to catch him to say hello and chat. I loved doing that because Wilfred knew the history of Paquette Road and always told good stories in his hybrid English-French Canadian accent.

One day Wilfred stopped to say hello and as we were talking about the house, the road, and the neighborhood, I asked him what used to be in the field where the *terrain de boules* was. He said that there was a barn and cows. I immediately asked him, "How did the cows drink?" He said that somewhere up in the field on the pond side of the road above where we were standing there was a spring.

After we parted ways I ran to the house like a madman, screaming that there was a spring up in the field. I assembled the kids and announced that we were going to find water. We started walking up the hill and I told the kids to spread out and keep a sharp lookout. It must have looked like a scene from an old French Marcel Pagnol movie, where people roam through the hills and meadows looking for springs. Of course I had no idea what a spring looked like in Vermont – was it just water coming out of the ground?

We kept walking until the kids started screaming, "We found something!" Right behind some bushes that we had previously passed a million times was a large cement cylinder with a cover made of two pieces of metal. I lifted the cover and peered down. Inside was water, and indeed the ground around the cylinder was damp.

I started researching and asking people about springs and how they worked, considering that we were in an area where the temperature fell to thirty degrees below zero in the winter. Wells such as these were generally at least ten feet deep, and the pipe taking the water out is below the freezing line. They have gravel at the bottom and an overflow hole close to the top. So in theory what we needed to do was to dig around the spring and try to find the pipe that had been previously used. Then (in my imagination) I would find a hose or some kind of pipe and take it all the way downhill to the pond, 800 feet away.

As it seemed to happen many times, out of thin air a solution soon presented itself. At this time we had started to explore the land and particularly the logging road that winds through the woods and comes back up through the front field. The logging road was a total mess – just to walk along it we had to wear waterproof boots, and the combination of water, bugs, and mud made it an unpleasant experience. One area in particular had a permanent swamp right in the middle of it. Driving the Gator over the road felt like a ride through Jurassic Park, and many times we were stuck in the mud and had to winch our way out. The first part of the road closest to the house had also stumps right in the middle of the road, which made it even more difficult to navigate.

We were told that if we had a logging road damaged by erosion we could apply to the Department of Agriculture and Wildlife in Newport, Vermont and get funding to rehabilitate it. We drove to Newport and met with two really nice people at the department. Then the department's expert visited the farm, and unfortunately he decided that our road did not qualify. (I don't know if anyone ever qualifies.) So that we could use the road to walk and bike and to give us easy access to the rest of the land, we decided to fix it ourselves. The goal was to be able to just walk through it without having to feel that we were going on a safari.

Eric Nichols and the Logging Trail

I mentioned the condition of the logging trial to Harry, and one day he took me to take a look at a project he was working on in Greensboro. We parked the truck on the side of the road and walked up a newly built dirt road. As we walked I noticed that the new road was perfectly smooth – it did not even have any marks of the teeth of the bucket from the excavator. Harry introduced me to Eric Nichols, who looked very much like his brother Chris Nichols. Eric is an excavator operator (isn't everybody in Vermont?) and could do magic with his machine – what he had done on Harry's road project was incredible. Harry said this guy is a master and he has been doing this for thirty years. Eric was working in three feet of mud and yet made it look easy and the end result was amazing. By then I knew some of the excavation jargon and felt more confident than when I had spoken to his brother Chris. And because Eric was referred to me by Harry, I had no doubts as to his skill and honesty. We agreed to meet at our place so he could look at the logging road. The logging road was a mile long and I was worried about cost.

The following week Eric came and we walked the logging road together and I urged him to see what he could do to make the road dry and flat for a walk or a bike ride. He kept reminding me that the road was very wet. That meant that water had to be somehow drained away from the road or under it. The inaccessibility of the logging road was weighing on me and I really wanted to be done so we could take a walk on it at any time without any Wellies or swamp attire.

Eric agreed that he could do the job but he couldn't tell how much time some sections would take to fix, so he couldn't give me a fixed price. I wanted the job done and I had faith that Eric was a man of his word. We gave him the OK.

He started work on a Tuesday and worked for a whole week. Every day I would walk up to the logging road to say hello and check on his progress. He quickly turned the logging road into a nice wide path. In some areas he had to raise the road so the water could drain, and in two spots he had to put pipes under the road to let the water flow downhill.

Our Version of the Roman Aqueducts

Meanwhile, I was still thinking about the dry pond and the newly discovered spring. Before Eric was done with the logging road, I asked him to dig a trench close to the spring to see if we could find a pipe. We walked around to see where to do it and he showed me an old trick. You can take two pieces of fern, bend them, and whisk them around, and if they part that is a sign that there is water. That particular day was too windy so we could not test the theory.

Sixty feet away from the spring Eric dug the first trench and found nothing. We decided to try closer to the spring – but not too close – and dug another trench and did not find anything. Lamia and the kids were getting ready to leave to have dinner at Claire's, a local restaurant in Hardwick. I was losing hope but asked Eric to try once more, very close to the spring.

He dug for a few minutes and then he suddenly stopped. I went over and saw a small black pipe sticking out of the dirt and water was flowing out of it and quickly creating a puddle. I was very excited but had to go to dinner with my family. It then occurred to me that if we left it as it was, the hole would fill up with water and I would not be able to reach the pipe. I asked Eric to open the trench towards the woods so the water could flow out. I thanked him and joined my family for dinner.

After dinner I returned with the kids to see what was going on. The water was flowing and the excitement was high.

The next morning I woke up at 5:30 am and rushed out to the spring. Now a new obsession took over: how to get the water to the pond. We went to Country Home Center, the Ace Hardware store in Morrisville, and presented our dilemma. (Every time I was stuck doing something and Harry was not around to help, we asked the crew at Country Home Center, and what loomed as a gargantuan dilemma for me in most cases was a simple answer to them). So they said, sure we have black plastic piping, how much do you need? When I said I needed

800 feet, I expected them to send me packing. But without batting an eye they handed me two rolls of 400 feet each. After buying some connecting rings and other hardware, we rushed back to the spring with high hopes.

We unrolled the two pipes and laid them on the ground from the pond up the hill to the spring, then connected the pipe to the spring. We were using walkie-talkies and I kept radioing the kids, "Is the water flowing?" Again and again the answer was, "No!" We were so close to success and my frustration started to show – I needed this project done, and now!

I surveyed the hill and right before the pond – covered by the second section of pipe – there is a small rise that I had assumed would not be a problem as long as the open end of the pipe was low enough. I lifted the pipe to give it more gravity, but it didn't do any good and as I fussed with it my team members were losing their enthusiasm.

I needed to analyze the problem. To see if the water was flowing through the first section from the spring, I disconnected the two sections of pipe. I observed that water was indeed flowing through the first section, but every time I connected it to the second section the flow stopped. I decided to move the second section of pipe to the other side of the field to make the uphill rise almost level. I assumed that the water needed to push the air out of the pipe and that once the water began to flow I could move the pipe back. I connected it and heard the joyful scream from the kids – "The water's flowing!"

This was a very exciting moment. After pushing the pipe back to the edge of the woods so it was out of view we attached the open end to the ladder of the floating dock. The water, which was cold enough to create condensation on the pipe, never stops flowing – at night we can even hear it from the terrace. As if that were the last piece to the puzzle, the sound of water flowing provided a beautiful bucolic sense of tranquility and completeness to our new property.

The Land and Forest

Into the Wild Woods

When we first saw the farm in May of 2008, our initial visits to the house were made during mud season and both days were rainy so at that time we did not inspect the property. Elizabeth Edgerton called it the "Hundred-Acre-Woods," like in *Winnie-the-Pooh*. I had no idea of surface area and I thought that one hundred acres was good enough and maybe even a bit small – maybe, but not really sure. The Edgertons also mentioned that there were trails through the woods, there was a small bridge somewhere in the woods that crossed a stream, and a logging road went through the woods and came out through the lower field.

We were in a kind of a haze and didn't register any of this, and during the first two months of ownership we didn't venture into the woods. We were new to the area and the forest seemed dense and foreboding. That summer was a very wet summer so we kept our activities around the house – and we did not really want to venture into the great unknown. The Norway spruce trees behind the house were overgrown and the branches reached to the ground and created a wall. No one dared go past the wall until we cut the branches to open up the woods.

Our dog Java started marking her territory and expanding her area of influence much faster than we did.

One day we finally mustered some courage and followed the logging road through the mud and mosquitoes to where it came out on the lower field. It felt as if we had gone bushwhacking. The logging road was muddy and swampy and was blocked by a lot of dead trees. We started finding the ribbons that marked the various trails Elizabeth had mentioned. The logging road was marked with blue. The trail that went to the hardwoods was red and the trail that left from behind the cottage was green. To me it felt as if we were conquering uncharted territory. I was worried about getting lost, especially if I went alone, so I ordered a set of walkie-talkies that worked like a charm.

In the local Hardwick *Gazette* Lamia saw an advertisement for an estate auction and she knew that I loved auctions so we piled the kids in the car and went looking for the location. We found a field where people had parked their cars and a tent with a large number of people who were used to attending auctions and had brought their own chairs. My guess was that many of the attendees were antiques dealers looking for deals, as well as some locals. A lot of pickup trucks and some larger trucks were parked outside the tent – clearly people were ready to take their items on the spot. We walked around the items that were for sale and spotted a few things of interest, but with the three kids we were limited to small purchases that could fit in the back of the Volvo. We bought two American Girl dolls for Leslie, a red rolling workshop chest of drawers, and last, to my pleasure, a set of hunting knives that were perfect for protection in the woods. I really wanted to buy more items but Lamia would not let me. We were still new to the area and not resourceful enough to figure out a way to get things to the house. One man had bought six dining room chairs for a ridiculously low price. With great interest I watched to see how he was going to lug his prizes away from the auction. He put three chairs in the trunk, with half the chairs sticking out of the trunk, and then he flipped one chair and put it through the window of the back – again with half the chair sticking out – and did the same to the front right window and the other back window. After taking his shoelaces out of his shoes, he tied the chairs to the car as best as he could.

Back home, I dedicated a drawer in the kitchen island to the knives. And now, before we go for a walk in the woods, I ask, "Who wants a knife?"

and the kids love to open the drawer and select a knife.

As summer came – after we had owned the house for nearly a year – I still did not feel that it was *our* land. Now that I had much more courage and various weapons, I was ready to explore the woods and gain a stronger understanding of the property. The boys and I started to copy the dog and everywhere we went on our land we would pee to mark our territory.

Finding the Corners

With the closing documents we had been given a forestry plan – a twenty-five-page document describing in great detail the forests and various trees on what was exactly 108 acres. The document was written by a man by the name of Ross Morgan. The document also had drawings and maps. Trying to make sense of it all, I spent a lot of time looking at the document and at Google Earth. The land had red and white pine, some Norway spruce, an area of mixed growth, and deep in the woods an area of hardwoods – mostly maple trees – that were, according to the document, really nice. We also learned that the land was marked on all corners.

The first step was to try and get in touch with the forester Ross Morgan. I called him and mentioned that we had bought the Edgerton's house and wanted to talk about forestry. Ross informed me that he was almost retired and did not really take on more work and that a younger man by the name of David McManus was the man I needed. I thanked Ross and hung up. For the time being, I shelved that part of the forestry, knowing that there was nothing really urgent in terms of document update.

I took on the challenge of finding the corners of the land. Our neighbor Neil Barclay proposed to walk the land with me to show me the trails. I took him up on his offer and off we went. We followed the first trail, which twisted and turned and was blocked by some fallen trees until we reached a swamp and a small stream over which someone had built a small log bridge. The land then sloped upward and the trees started to change from pine and spruce to a mix, and then to sugar maples. The change was dramatic and I found myself in a full maple forest that admitted enough dappled light to make it feel kind of magical. I was in awe and could not wait to tell Lamia and the kids. We kept walking and found double red ribbons that, as I later learned, marked the boundary of the land. We finished our walk and I thanked Neil for his help.

The next day we all went looking for the corners. Everyone came including the dog and we brought snacks and of course the knives for protection. It felt as if we were going on an adventure, not just exploring our backyard. I showed them the way and when we got to the maple forest my family felt the same way I had: this place was magical. Sitting quietly in a clearing, surrounded by old maple trees, soft light illuminating the understory, the soul felt somehow rested and the world a little more balanced.

The land is shaped like a reversed "L" so we were looking for the tip of the bottom part of the L. I assumed that the trail turned somewhere close to the end of the land so all we had to do was get off the trail, spread out, and start looking. We found more double red ribbons, which meant that we were at the edge of the land, and we followed that line until we found what we were looking for.

At the base of a large tree was a steel rod with a small red flag. This was very exciting – we had found the far corner of the land! To mark our territory, the boys both peed near (but not *on*) the flag.

We then followed the trail back to the logging road and the house. The sensation was like nothing I had felt before – we had found the hidden boundary of our land. On our way back to the house on the logging road we all stopped in front of a tree that became a landmark. It defied gravity by growing first vertically then for some reason turned downward then turned again and regained a vertical aim. We later learned that this was due to ice damage.

Ross Morgan, the Tree Whisperer

We still needed to meet the author of our forestry plan and get his input. We read in the Hardwick *Gazette* that Ross Morgan was giving a tour of a swamp near his house and that he was regarded as an expert in his field. My first attempt to talk to him had failed so I asked Harry if I should try to work with Ross and he said that Ross was the best, but that he was very busy.

We had time to wait. So for the next nine months we exchanged messages and Ross said that he would drop by sometime. I told Lamia to make sure to interrupt anything I was doing if a man by the name of Ross Morgan came by the house.

One summer day our dog Java started barking furiously. I put down my lunch and opened the mudroom door to see a man who looked like Santa Claus wearing khaki clothes with blue paint marks.

The man said, "Hello, I'm Ross Morgan."

I almost choked and at the same time it felt like Christmas. I told him not to go anywhere while I found my boots – I was afraid that he would disappear.

He looked at me and said, "Let's take a walk."

I called Lamia and the kids and we walked around the house and we started some of the nicest most instructive walks around our land. Ross knew the Edgertons well and was a wealth of knowledge on local trees and stories. From then on when Ross came to the house I was always so pleased to see him and looked forward to our walks and always learned something new.

I soon found out that Ross not only looks like Santa Claus, but he is just as nice and brings as much joy to the people around him. I learned that when Ross came back from the war Phillip Edgerton helped him find a job, and for this Ross is forever grateful. Ross also loved talking to the kids when they would come along for the walks. We learned all about red and white pine, Norway spruce, and about thinning and marking trees. He had such respect and love for nature and trees that it was infectious and he loved to transfer his knowledge to whoever was interested. He was semi-retired and carefully picked his projects, and we felt grateful that he agreed to work with us.

We had several projects in mind including updating the forestry plan, thinning parts of the forest, and clearing an area for agriculture. One day Ross dropped by with photos of his brother, a friend, and himself building a log cabin. This was an intriguing new idea and we immediately resolved to build one deep in the woods. The following day he dropped off books on various log cabin designs and how to build one. But reality intruded; there were not enough hours in the day or days in the week to do every project. We keep that one on the back burner.

A lot of the pine trees on the land were planted in the 1950s in rows, and our goal was to thin them in a way to recreate the sense of random planting. Ross had a special kind of spray

paint and would walk backward and spray a
dot on the tree that he thought should be cut.
By walking backward he could see all the dots
and have a general view.

Chris Daniels, Vermont's Paul Bunyan

The next step was to find a reputable logger. A lot of people in the area call themselves loggers, especially in the winter off-season when other work is not available, so you have to be careful. Ross recommended a fellow by the name of Chris Daniels. Ross said that Chris was very nice, very honest, and worked on his own with minimal impact on the land – no large machines. He also had two workhorses that he used in dense forests where his tractor couldn't get in. Ross said that one time he recommended Chris to a family in the area and they kept working with Chris for a long time doing all kinds of projects including logging, cutting firewood, and building cabins and bridges. Ross said that he would ask Chris to drop by one day to meet me.

This is how business is done in rural Vermont – you don't just call up a builder or logger or excavator and make an appointment for a consultation in their air-conditioned office. You pass word through the grapevine, and if the vibe is right the person you want to meet will eventually appear at your door.

One day we were relaxing on the stone terrace. Java started barking – a flatbed truck was in the driveway. Out of the truck stepped a very tall and very large man with a grey beard and overalls. Ross had mentioned that Chris was the nicest guy and that he was big. The kids looked at Chris and thought that he was a giant.

Chris introduced himself. He spoke very softly and slowly. It was the same deal as practically everyone who worked with us; I asked him if he could cut trees and he replied yes, he could – the ones that Ross marked.

We walked around for a while and I told him to go ahead and start anytime he wanted, but if he needed to work close to the house I needed to know so the kids would stay away.

The first field Chris started clearing became known in the family as the Chris Daniels Field. Every day I would drive the Gator with the kids to say hello and look at the progress. I could sit and watch Chris working for hours. I tried once to imitate him. I managed to cut down a small tree and I realized how skilled he was and how heavy trees are. He wields a chainsaw like a child holding a small plastic toy.

One day he asked me what my plans were for the next day and I said that I was going to take the kids to the Lamoille Valley Fair, near Johnson. We often visit Johnson to go to one of the few independent bookstores – Lamia and the kids love poking around in bookstores. Johnson is also home to one of our favorite restaurants in the area, the Winding Brook Bistro. The restaurant is a small house on the side of the road with a really nice ambiance, local artwork on the walls, and a simple but creative menu. We would often go there as a treat after a long day of work. We took our good friends Zeina and Fadi, who with their two girls Sascha and Raya had come all the way from Lebanon to visit. Boy, was that a different experience for them.

The fair was your typical rural attraction with rides, shooting games, and tents selling all kinds of local artifacts. We bumped into Chris, who was there for a horse-pulling competition, and we also watched a truck-pulling competition. For me, this was real America, and in fact right on the edge of the Craftsbury Common there is a poignant memorial to the soldiers from Craftsbury who died during World War II.

Clearing and Digging

During a very hot week in July I had Chris the logger cutting wood and Eric fixing the logging road with his big yellow excavator. I felt good. Watching them work brought back childhood memories of standing at the window of my parents' apartment watching roadwork or the construction of a building next door.

At the end of each day I would go with the kids to see the progress on the logging road. Eric was covering a lot of distance, putting a ditch here and a culvert there as if he were playing with a toy. Every time I asked him how were things, he would say it is wet and hot. The poor man was working in ninety-five-degree heat at full throttle. Seeing the logging road getting fixed and cleared felt like having a very stuffy nose for a long time and one day it all clears and you can breathe again.

After five days Eric was done and the logging road looked great – an accessible open road through the woods for a one-mile loop. I began the enjoyable habit of walking the loop alone or with family, and the best conversations with my kids happened on the logging road.

Before Eric disappeared with his machine he did two smaller projects – to clear and level an area next to the growing strips that we had cleared, and help me find the pipe coming out of the spring we had found. These two items were no problem and he was done a day later. Eventually the yellow machine was taken away by the man who moves all the machines in the area. It costs money to move an excavator so the ritual is that the machine stays on site until it gets moved to the next job, therefore only costing a one-time travel charge to each client.

Eric had done the logging road job during a very hot and rainless period that had lasted a few weeks. A week after he left we experienced a twenty-four-hour rainfall that poured down an incredible amount of rain in just one day – some said eight inches but some reports had numbers as high as sixteen inches. I had just seeded the logging road with conservation mix (a quick grass cover used to repair damaged slopes and excavated sites) containing Kentucky bluegrass, ryegrass, clover, and fescue (a shade-tolerant, cool-season grass) designed to hold the ground and avoid erosion. Early in the morning I walked to the logging road to see if it had eroded. To my horror one of the drainage pipes Eric had installed could not handle the amount of water and a small section of the road had flooded, washing away a lot of my seeds and part of the road. Another section was also very wet and the water had not drained as planned. "Breaking ditches" are small swales in the middle of the dirt logging road designed to avoid water rushing and building strength down the hill, redirecting water away from the road roughly every thirty yards. The same concept is used on regular dirt roads used by cars; ditches along the sides of the roads on hills usually have culverts or just breaking points to push the water into a field; otherwise full-fledged torrents could build up.

We also learned – the hard way – that the town

of Craftsbury owned, and is responsible for, the land from the middle of Paquette Road to a distance of fifteen feet on each side. Near the pond and the *terrain de boules* we had planned to grow a meadow-like area to create a natural fence. We carefully watched the meadow grow and then we mowed a small section near the road to get the effect – mowed, overgrown, and then back to mowed. One day when the meadow had grown to five feet high I was standing in the driveway and heard a loud machine coming up the road. At first I thought that it might be John Bailey driving his tractor to the fields above, but I soon saw that it was very large and had a long arm sticking out of the side to which was attached a rectangular base, as if the tractor were sweeping the roadside. By the time I figured out what was going on it was too late. This was the town tractor mowing the sides of all the roads to avoid overgrowth, and in thirty seconds it had wiped out my beloved meadow. For the first time in Vermont I was astonished – how could this man do such a thing?

Heartbroken and laughing at the same time, I stood there and saw that the view to the other side of the road was now clear. A few minutes later I heard the same noise but this time it was coming back down along the other side of the road doing the same thing. I wanted to talk to the guy so I jumped in his path, waving for him to stop. He stopped and turned off the engine so we could hear each other. I asked him if he knew what he had done. He looked clueless and I decided not to give him a hard time, so I told him not to worry about it.

He said next time put a sign saying, "Don't mow." Good idea! So we added a sign to our collection of signs – DON'T MOW, SLOW DOWN – CHILDREN AT PLAY, and HUNTING SAFETY ZONE. I was crushed that my meadow was gone, but it reminded me that Gilbert had also parked his excavator in another meadow that I was letting grow wild. I realized that wild meadows are everywhere, and how were the town employees supposed to know that on the advice of our landscape architects we were using them as design elements?

So we had finally cleared land for agriculture, filled the pond, fixed the logging road, and found some of the corners of the property – now we were ready for some action.

Bird Stories

Teacup was the name we gave a turkey that showed up every day at around 5:00 pm and walked around the house and fields. I once saw Teacup as I was mowing, and will admit to giving the engine full throttle to catch it – but Teacup was too fast, and it could also fly.

Once we saw eight huge wild turkeys all sitting in a small crab apple tree across from the house eating the apples. It looked as if it were a turkey tree. I wanted to scare them with the BB gun but Lamia did not let me.

The next day we saw a great blue heron fly down and land right next to the pond. We tried to slowly walk down to get closer but kids are very noisy scouts and the heron flew away. We saw it many times after that.

On another occasion a seagull came to visit. I walked past it and I thought that the bird looked like a seagull, but what would a seagull be doing around here? I never liked them because they were very aggressive due to the fact that people fed them on the beach. Once on the beach in Rhode Island a seagull even grabbed a sandwich out of Lamia's hand.

I looked at it, and it looked at me. We both were wondering what was going

on. A seagull in the middle of Vermont? The only possibility was that either it was migrating and got lost – but I did not think that seagulls migrated – or the other option was that lakes had seagulls and it came from one of the nearby lakes.

A couple of days passed and the seagull was till there and gaining confidence. It grabbed an apple I had thrown after taking a couple of bites to try it. We tried to shoo it away, without results. As they say in French, *"Aux grands mots les grands moyens"* (Desperate times call for desperate measures). I told the kids that they could take their BB gun and try to shoot it to scare it away. Henry and James were very excited but Leslie did not want to harm the bird. I told her that the BBs would not hurt the bird. The two boys went out for their first hunting experience. The funny thing was that the seagull was not afraid of people and it just stood there. They missed a bunch of times and hit it a couple of times but it just moved a few feet.

The rest of the story will remain untold as it is unclear whether hunting seagulls is legal in Vermont.

The Deed

When you move into a new house that has just been built, you know that you are the very first people to live there. But when you buy an old house in a tightly knit community, you soon learn to appreciate the richness of the property's heritage. Chances are good that some of your neighbors have a direct and personal connection to your house. Others before you have called the place home, and it is likely that many years from now some other family will create their own memories. You aren't an owner of the property so much as you are a temporary caretaker.

The dirt roads of Vermont are very punishing to cars and especially to the tires. In one summer we had three flat tires and each time we would go to Denton Auto Repair, conveniently located near our farm on Wild Branch Road. One day, Lamia was waiting for the tire to be fixed and the owner Mike Denton commented to her that his mother was born in our house.

We already knew that Harry and Steve Moffet used to party in the house, and Neil lived in it while building his own house up the road. Plus there was the old shoe that Phillip Edgerton had found in the house. All of these things together with Mike's comment to Lamia motivated me to dig deeper and find out more about the history of the house and the families who lived there.

I called the town clerk's office and spoke to Betty Cheril and also to Yvette. Yvette agreed to meet us in the town clerk's office on a Sunday and to help us find all the deeds to the house. I offered the kids a financial reward for helping, and on the appointed Sunday we all sat in the office examining deeds in reverse chronological order. This is not an easy task. Every deed has the name of the grantee and the grantor and a reference to another large binder for the previous deed. As we went back in time things became more difficult because the documents were written in the old-school cursive and the kids could not read it. Also, the deeds reflected the status of the land but did not mention if the

house or any other houses were on the property.
Here's what we discovered.

Rocambole Farm Deeds

Date	Owner
[....]	Edward Foster
[....]	[....]
[....]	Harriet A. Hoyt, Widow
6/15/1912	Clarence H. and Jennie Lowell
6/30/1951	Willis A. Lowell and Marion V. Lowell
	With one surge two-single unit milking machine and pump
	4 can milk cooler
	1 Oliver Sulky plow
	1 Clark Cutaway harrow
	1 McCormick-Deering new horse dump rake
	1 six-foot cut McCormick-Deering mowing machine
	No. 10 horse drawn New Idea manure spreader
	One horse plow and cultivator
	1 rubber-tired wagon
	One pair two-horse logging sleds
	One wheelbarrow with rubber tires

	One hayfork and track
	One 3-year-old Guernsey cow
6/26/1953	Clarence H. and Jennie Lowell
	All of the above minus the cow
9/12/1956	Jerome Y. Lettvin and wife and Alfred Holland and wife
6/13/1960	Alfred and Taffy Holland to Jerome Y. and Margaret Lettvin
6/21/1989	Henry and Patricia Coe
2/19/1999	Phillip and Elizabeth Edgerton
6/27/2008	Lamia and Ziad Moukheiber

As we reviewed the various deeds we noticed that all the transactions except two were made in June, including ours, as if we were all meant to be linked to one another.

While in the town clerk 's office we looked at the original town map and finally understood why the town was called Craftsbury. Many of the residents on the map had the last name Craft along with very interesting first names including Lucretia, Ebenezer, Mehitabel, and Griffine.

The Farm

Nature's Bounty

Once during a visit to France we were having dinner with some friends in the small Provence village of Saint Saturnin-les-Apts. While we were having drinks our host offered us a plate of tomatoes with *fleur de sel* (sea salt harvested from the top layer of the salt marsh) and olive oil harvested from their olive trees. We then walked to his yard and cut some fresh basil.

The following day we paid a visit to relatives in Carpentras, near Avignon, and our host picked some basil from the garden and pounded it into a pesto paste (or *pistou*, which in the Provençal language means "pounded") to be served in the *soupe au pistou.*

I was envious and resolved that growing our own food would be my goal. For so many people in the United States – and, increasingly, even in Provence – the experience of growing, cooking, and appreciating our own food is a lost art, and we live a life of processed food and hectic pace.

At our newly acquired farm in Vermont, when the landscaping was done we began the farming plans. Lamia was knowledgeable about gardening, but neither of us knew much about growing food crops.

Charlie Proutt and Tricia had helped us by planning for three eighty-foot-long-and-ten-feet-wide beds at the back of the house. They showed us how to grow on narrow strips with walkways going across, and how raised beds are easier to weed because we have to bend less, and how they provide more room for deeper roots to grow. Raised beds also allow for walkways to get compacted, resulting in fewer weeds, but the beds never get stepped on. The soil retains all of its air and pathways created by the beneficial activity of earth worms. Who knew?

We ordered a large amount of compost for these beds and it took us two days to haul it and spread it. Anners also used compost for her beds, and the consensus was not to use bark mulch, which according to her disrupts the composition of the soil. So after an arduous couple of days of backbreaking labor, we had three long beds and smaller strip right next to the kitchen ready to be seeded with our hearts' desire.

What should we plant? We decided to split the growing into two sections, one for personal consumption and the other for commercial sale.

For personal consumption we started doing research and making a list of vegetables that we would like to eat. In our research we came across High Mowing Organic Seeds, a local company that happens to be less than five miles away and is owned by a gentleman by the name of Tom Stearns. Lamia, who is occasionally obsessed with buying locally, was thrilled. Tom had started tinkering with seeds in his back yard as a boy and later expanded his idea into one of the largest businesses in the region, selling seeds all around the country. He has a passion for the Northeast Kingdom and was one of the main people who helped the town of Hardwick reinvent itself as a center for sustainable agriculture. He joined forces with other business owners in the area to create a center to develop all kinds of new sustainable projects. We ordered all our seeds from him and later got to know Heather, one his employees who would recommend the best varieties and things we would like such as the Mediterranean cucumbers or *Ronde de Nice* squash.

We did not know anything about either growing vegetables for our own use or growing for commercial sale. The approach I took is to choose things I liked to eat and have had a great impact on my palate.

The first item I thought of was garlic. It's legendary throughout the Mediterranean and is a key ingredient in many of my favorite dishes.

Like many urban people, I loved garlic but I thought that it came in just one variety – the kind you find in the little cellophane package in the supermarket.

I had no idea how to grow garlic, so I started my research. The first thing I discovered was that garlic has many varieties. I found a garlic seed vendor in the Seattle area and called them to learn more about the varieties they sold and the differences between each variety.

There are two basic types of garlic plant. Hardneck types *(Allium sativum ophioscorodon)* usually send up a flower stalk. They grow well in climates with very cold winters, producing large cloves that are easy to peel. The *ophios* include five true hardneck varieties (Porcelain, Rocambole, Purple Stripe, Marbled Purple Stripe, and Glazed Purple Stripe) and three weakly bolting hardnecks that often produce softnecks (Creole, Asiatic, and Turban).

Softneck garlic *(Allium sativum sativum)* grows well in a wide range of conditions. The skins of softnecks are tighter, so they store better over longer periods. Softnecks have two varieties, Silverskin and Artichoke. Supermarket garlic is almost all Silverskin garlic from China or California. Silverskins can be planted mechanically and are good keepers.

Over time, individual garlic plants adapt to the soil and climate where they are cultivated. Of these ten varieties, there are as many as 600 sub-varieties that reflect a mysterious blend of genetics and local growing conditions.

Garlic can grow from its own cloves – if you take one bulb or head of garlic and separate all the cloves and then take those and plant them, each one will give you a full head of garlic. I learned that in Vermont, garlic needs to be planted in late October – roughly four weeks prior to the ground freezing – so it grows a small sprout and then goes dormant for the rest of the winter. The beds needed to be covered with straw or hay to avoid frost damage to the sprouts. The first time around I ordered the following eight varieties of garlic and patiently waited for October to get my shipment of seed.

Idaho Silver (Silverskin)

Okrent (Artichoke)

Chesnok Red (Purple Stripe)

Silver White (Silverskin)

Purple Glazer (Glazed PS)

Burgundy (Creole)

Xian (Turban)

Polish Hardneck (Porcelain)

I was learning my first lesson of growing any type of crop – understanding and mastering the art of patience. As they say in farming business, there is always next year. If your crop of vegetables survives the freezing cold winter, it might get eaten by deer. If it survives that, it could catch a fungus. If *that* doesn't kill it, voles burrowing underground might get it, and if you're not careful you can mow over it. Another huge lesson was the dandelions – if you don't cut them before they flower, you triple your weeding work.

Gators and Tractors and Mowers

Another unknown area for me was machinery. I was a total stranger to tractors, mowers, and other farm equipment; the most mechanical thing I had ever used was a push snowblower.

When we had first visited the farm Phil Edgerton had showed me his bright blue New Holland tractor. I did not know what to make of it. At the time I thought that tractors were cheap and I was sure that the Edgertons would simply include the tractor as part of the house. When they offered to sell it to me for ten thousand dollars I thought it was lot of money and I passed on the offer. I later found that this was a big mistake – the New Holland was a really nice tractor and would have been perfect for our property and we should have bought it.

After we had bought the farm and I realized that we had to get something, I agonized over the equipment we needed – mower, a tractor, a small utility vehicle? I called John Deere and presented my predicament, and they kept asking me what I needed and how large was my operation. I was really confused. As far as the tractor went, I found that they were in fact very expensive and came in many different models and varieties for different tasks. How many horsepower did I want? What kind of hydraulics? Did I need a power takeoff (PTO) accessory for running other implements? Even tires are complicated – did I want turf tires, "ag" tires, or R4?

I finally figured out a good combination: a ride-on mower for the grass around the house, which came out to around three acres, and a John Deere Gator to drive around the land and carry items and dirt if needed. Because tractors and mowers are vehicles for just one person, the green Gator, which resembles a compact Jeep with fat tires and a roll cage, would allow me to also take the kids.

A truck showed up one day and delivered the mower and the Gator and the delivery guy showed me how to use them. This was love at first sight! The Gator and mower became my best friends and the kids once asked me if I loved the Gator more than them. My answer was, "I love you all equally."

The kids started to learn to drive the Gator – something that at their ages would be unimaginable in Boston but is routine in rural Vermont. We found a small field uphill from the house and called it the Gator lesson spot. They loved driving it and became really good. I also tied a thick cotton rope to the back so when kids are sitting in the dump area they can hold on to something.

But familiarity can breed carelessness. Once I put the kids in the back of the Gator along with some saws and large pruning shears. We hit a bump and one of the kids came down on the saw – fortunately without injury. I learned that with "Gator freedom" also comes "greater responsibility."

The mower was great. I never understand why therapists don't recommend to their patients to go mow a couple of acres of land. Mowing while wearing headphones is one of the most therapeutic things I have ever done.

My oldest child Henry wanted to use the mower, but the seat has an automatic kill switch designed to shut off the engine if the driver falls off the seat. Henry was not heavy enough to keep the kill switch from activating, so we stuffed his pockets with stones to try to weigh him down. It worked, and with bulging pockets he started racing the mower around while the other two kids took the Gator and drove around the grassy area around the house. Lamia and I insisted that the two kids in the Gator had to have their seat belts on, and no one could get off either machine unless all machines were turned off. They had a blast.

We also invented a game called "para-rescue jumping." The kids would stand in the side passenger area of the Gator while I drove it fairly fast to a sloping section of the grass. I would yell, "Jump!" and the kids would jump out of the Gator pretending to be parachute jumpers. They jumped and rolled on the grass.

Once I had decided on the mower and Gator,

the big next step was a chain saw. I called John Deere and they sent me a small chainsaw, but at that same time I mentioned it to Harry and he said that I also needed chaps, a helmet, steel-toed boots, and gloves. His detailed descriptions of horrific chainsaw accidents put fear and doubt in my mind and I immediately ordered all the necessary protection.

My first project was to prune an apple tree. I donned my gladiator gear: an orange hat with a grill for face protection, orange Kevlar chaps, huge steel-toed boots, and gloves. All of this to cut one branch. I successfully cut the branch and I decided that the time I spent gearing up was longer than if I had simply used a handsaw, so from then on I rarely used the chainsaw. I was too scared to use it and I knew that at any point in time a kid could pop out behind me. We spent a lot of time teaching the kids about the necessary distance to stay away from any person working. They could not walk up to me from behind, stick their head right at my waist, and say, "What are you doing, daddy?" A couple of times I had hit them in the head because I was using a handsaw and going back and forth.

As we were getting to know the world of agriculture we discovered that the area was booming with activity and energy in the local and sustainable food world. The town of Hardwick in particular had businesses that were driving the effort and they all collaborated in an association called the Center for an Agricultural Economy. They hosted seminars, courses, and various other activities to help the community. Right next door to the Center on Main Street in Hardwick was Claire's Restaurant. Claire's was started with the help of the community; fifty people invested $1,000 each and in return each received a monthly discount of $25 at the restaurant. Claire's used only local products and was slowly becoming a destination for people from all over the area.

The main businesses that were leading the charge in the organic, local, and sustainable agriculture were High Mowing Seeds, Pete's Greens, Jasper Hill Farm, and Vermont Soy.

They were all exciting businesses with very dynamic owners. We met two of them, Tom Stearns and Pete Johnson.

John Bailey's Cows

One of the high points of many days for the kids was to jump in the Gator and drive down to John Bailey's organic farm to watch and help with milking the cows. John often drove his tractor up and down Paquette Road to cut hay or dump manure in his field. One day John stopped his tractor and introduced himself. Everyone talks about gentlemen farmers but here was a farmer who was a gentleman. He's one of the nicest men I have ever had the pleasure to know and one of the very few people I have ever met who pronounced my name correctly the first time.

John is a reticent Vermonter who becomes downright gregarious when asked about his cows. He was more than happy to share his knowledge with the kids and to let them operate the milking machinery. Because his is an organic operation, the cows cannot be given any antibiotics and therefore cleanliness is paramount. John showed the kids how to wipe down the teats twice with iodine, how never to use the same towel from one cow to the next, and finally how to affix the four-armed pump to the cows' teats. The children loved the vacuum sound each pump made when attached to the teat. You can't beat that for getting up close and personal with nature. All the while, a conveyer belt, cleverly positioned at the rear of the cows, was in perpetual motion carrying away the fresh manure and depositing it in the spreader.

John then showed us how the milk was sucked up into tubes that carried it to the holding tank. He showed us how we could get milk from the holding tank, and we filled a glass milk bottle for later tasting. Vermont farms are allowed to sell a small amount of raw milk (unpasteurized) directly to the consumer. There is a huge battle raging among milk aficionados about the benefits of raw milk, countered by the passionate pleas of the pro-pasteurization camp on the dangers of Listeria and other bacteria. The pros versus the cons of raw milk are outside the scope of this book; suffice it to say that we chose to defy conventional wisdom and for the first time taste raw milk, milked just a half-hour earlier. Back home, we gathered around the island, set out the glasses and each took a swig. For those of us accustomed to skim milk, raw whole milk is like dessert: sweet and thick and delicious!

Cheese

Every crop has a different schedule for seeding, growing, and harvesting, and one has to adapt and fill the calendar with different projects. So while I was waiting for the garlic seeds to arrive, I took on the challenge of making cheese. I drove down to John Bailey's with a crate full of glass milk bottles and filled them directly from John's milk tank. Late in the afternoon he would be milking the cows and the milk could not be any fresher. I would keep track of what I took and I'd pay him at a later date.

I first learned how to turn milk into yogurt by boiling it to the right temperature and letting it cool down. After introducing live cultures and turning the milk into yogurt, I drained it for two days and added some salt. Then I made balls out of the hardened mixture and rolled them in a thyme mixture and stored them in small containers filled with olive oil. The cheese was delicious and fresh.

I discovered another pleasure – giving my product to guests and visitors so that every time anyone came to visit I made sure to give them cheese, vegetables, or anything we had made. The only items I never gave anyone – and will never give anyone – are the English shelling peas. I first discovered shelling peas as a kid in Lebanon; in the spring we would eat them uncooked as an *hors d'oeuvre* before a meal with a drink. When the first crop of shelling peas came out I was in heaven, reliving a childhood experience. They were a precious commodity around the house. I'd crack open the bright-green pea pods to find the lighter-green peas themselves inside. Shelling peas should be round, hearty-looking, and taste sweet and crunchy. I'd eat shelling peas out of hand, or spend a few minutes gathering a cup of peas and using them in pasta, salads, and countless other fresh preparations.

Growing Garlic

After what seemed to be an endless wait, in October the garlic seeds arrived and the family gathered around the vegetable bed to plant the first-ever crop at the farm. The kids brought the measuring tape and with surgical precision the garlic seeds were planted six inches apart. We spread the hay I had bought from John Bailey, and when it was all done we were obliged to patiently await the results the following summer.

One friend simply asked me, "Why don't you just buy garlic from the store?" Of course we did, but we were eagerly looking forward to harvesting our own.

When the thaw came the following spring, the garlic sprouts started showing. In the middle of the month of June, half of the crop started to grow a round, hard-looking shoot from the middle of the plant that grew straight up and then started to coil on itself. Thanks to Google I learned that these were called garlic scapes and came out of hardneck varieties only. They had to be cut so all the nutrients were sent to the bulb and not to the scape.

Another lesson of farming is that nothing gets wasted. I chopped the scapes into small pieces and sautéed them in a pasta sauce, and that night at dinner scapes entered our life and we loved them. They taste like garlic but milder and more "green." A good friend of mine named Julien, who loved my garlic, took some scapes and came up with a great way of using them. He put them in a blender and added olive oil and some herbs, salt, and pepper, and made a paste that can be used on meat for grilling, making garlic bread, or on a pizza. This recipe allowed me to use the scapes practically all year 'round; otherwise they would sit in the refrigerator, where real estate was at a premium.

In mid-July, over two years since we had first seen the house and farm, it was finally time to harvest our first garlic crop. The challenge, especially with kids helping, was to make sure that the varieties stayed separate, and as a new garlic farmer it was tough for me to tell the difference. We pulled them one by one, with some occasional casualties. Some bulbs were large and firm, while others were very small and did not do so well. The hardnecks were easier to pull out of the ground than the softnecks.

Once we had pulled them out of the ground we tied them in bundles and hung them to dry in the Shaker shed adjacent to the house. I was very proud of the garlic hanging in the shed and always showed them off to our guests. After the garlic was dried we sorted them in three categories: the seed garlic that we were going to replant next year, the ones we kept for our personal consumption and for friends and family, and the garlic for sale.

To try to make a sale, I called Claire's Restaurant in Hardwick and asked them if they wanted to buy some garlic, emphasizing that we were focused on varieties. I did not know whether to sell it by the piece or the weight; I thought that by the piece was easier but Steven the chef insisted on weight and asked for four pounds of each variety. I agreed and told him that we would deliver the next day.

I didn't have a scale to weigh the garlic. It was too late to go to Morrisville to buy one so I drove the Gator over to John Bailey's place and asked him if he had a scale. After rummaging around in his barn for a while, John emerged with a beat-up old scale and a three-pound dumbbell to help me adjust the scale so the weight would be accurate. While we were doing that, Chris Daniels the logger dropped by and saw us hovering over the scale with the dumbbell. With a chuckle he asked us if we were trying to sell marijuana. Apparently illicit marijuana growers are a huge problem in the region.

With the scale ready to go I rushed back home. While on the road Wilfred Paquette stopped to say hi from his car, and he asked that because of his respiratory problem if we would not burn any of the brush that Chris Daniels's logging was producing. I told him that I would see what I could do and told him not to tell his son Mark, a state weights and measures inspector, that

I was going to use an old scale to weigh the garlic. Perhaps we could work out a deal – he stays mum about the uninspected scale and I see about not burning the brush pile.

Back at the shed, working furiously to meet a late afternoon delivery deadline, Lamia and I weighed all the bags and made cute little "Rocambole Farm" tags describing each variety. That evening we delivered to Claire's Restaurant our first commercial crop of garlic. A few days later, I received the following email from Steven Obranovich, the chef at Claire's: "Really happy with the garlic! They all have varying degrees of heat or sharpness with equally interesting levels of sugar. Thanks so much for letting me be the guinea pig."

Wow! I almost can't believe that we pulled that off.

Endives

Our agriculture life was clearly not complicated enough so we started thinking of another crop that we could grow commercially alongside the garlic. We were looking for something that we liked, that was not popular, and that had a high profit margin; and we definitely did not want to compete with anyone locally. Lamia had the brilliant idea to grow Belgium endive. Endive is very popular in Europe and can be found everywhere, but in the United States they are relatively less well known and all the endive consumed here is mostly imported from Belgium, Holland, or Canada. The decision was made that endive was going to be the other crop. We would be a garlic-and-endive farm. Growing garlic was starting to become clear to us, but as far as endive was concerned we were totally in the dark (we later discovered the accuracy of the pun).

According to our research, a Belgian soldier who had in his basement some chicory root for making soup discovered endive. He was called to go to war, so he covered the roots and left. Upon his return he found that the roots had sprouted tender white leaves.

Producing endive is a two-step process. You first grow the endive plant normally, and then you uproot the plant and cut off the green leaves, leaving only the roots. You then replant the roots in moist soil and leave them in darkness. After a few weeks you harvest the tender pale white shoots.

I mentioned the plan to Harry, who was interested in this new crop. In his non-building and non-hunting life Harry also farmed, so we both went to visit High Mowing Seeds in Hardwick to meet with Tom Sterns to discuss our plan, and to see if they could help and if they had endive seeds. We parked the car outside High Mowing Seeds and went in to see Tom, who took us on a tour of his seed business that he had started in his backyard. I was impressed. We also talked to Heather, who is in charge of seed trials. We explained our plan and they were extremely helpful. We agreed to start an endive trial with three varieties.

The world of endive was coming into focus; we had figured out the plan to grow the seeds – but then what?

Heather recommended I contact a man by the name of Anthony Graham, of Temple-Wilton Community farm in southern New Hampshire, who grew endive locally for his farm members. I called Anthony and made an appointment and asked my colleague to drive me there. Heather was also going to meet us there. We met Anthony on his farm set amongst the rolling hills. There was a courtyard where on one side he had a retail store for his farm members, and on the other a barn and some other buildings. His farming philosophy was a biodynamic one, which is one step beyond organic and was too complicated for me to understand at the time. Anthony was very kind and showed us around and took us through the whole endive-growing process. His goal was to get endive ready for the Christmas season every year. If you only eat local and organic food in New England, once you get past the month of September green vegetables become rare and endive are welcome during the Christmas season.

After meeting with Anthony we had most of the theoretical knowledge we needed to get our plan in motion.

Harry also met with Pete Johnson, the brother of Anners the landscaper. We had heard a lot about him. Pete was a very energetic farmer who had graduated from Middlebury College, started his farm in Craftsbury, and was selling to the whole area. Pete was very nice and encouraging and offered to buy the endive for his CSA customers.

So by the end of the summer we had our roots ready. Now we had to figure out where to force our endive crop. We were a new operation and unsure of our prospects so we decided to hedge our bets and force the endive in our mudroom. It had a separate thermostat from the rest of the house, it was relatively small, and the few windows could be covered with thick black plastic. Harry started forcing them in December and in mid-January had the first batch ready. When the first endive sprouted and were ready, Harry took a photo with a ruler next to it and sent it to me as a birth announcement. We were ecstatic.

I came up to the house to check out our harvest. I picked some of the fresh endive in total darkness and gingerly took them to the kitchen to taste. Sprinkled with olive oil and some salt, they were heavenly. I was eating my own homegrown endive!

I asked Harry to take a sample to Steven at Claire's to see if the restaurant was interested. I did not hear anything back right away, but I said nothing because I didn't want to pester him.

A couple of weeks later I came up with Julien, who used to own a restaurant and who is a food specialist, and I asked Harry, Heather, and Tom Sterns to meet us for dinner at Claire's. We arrived at Claire's before everyone else and sat down at the table and had a drink. Then the bearded men showed up (in the winter most guys grow their beards because they work outdoors and facial hair helps with the cold). It was time to order dinner and Harry said to look at the menu. There was an endive-and-beet salad. Knowing that Claire's uses local produce, I was shocked that someone else was selling endive in the area.

Harry quickly rectified the confusion: this was our endive! I was so happy to see our endive on the menu I took a photo of the plate and took a menu home to keep as a souvenir of this event.

Our sense of accomplishment was tremendous. This was the culmination of a crazy plan that had started two years earlier on Mother's Day with a simple road trip to the Northeast Kingdom of Vermont.

The endive seed is extremely small – a gust of wind can blow it away. The experience of growing food from a tiny seed that keeps growing and then produces a vegetable that tastes so good is incredible. It needs to be nurtured and the seed needs to be planted in the most suitable place.

The dirt has to be of the right composition and compost and nutrients need to be added – not too much, not too little, and at the right time. During the first growth stage the plants need full sun at least seven hours a day. Rain is important for the growth process, but too much of it or too little of it are not so good. Then comes the weeding, a tedious and laborious process that has to be done continuously; if you ignore it for any length of time the weeds take over and stunt the growth of your plant. Then you have to protect your beloved plants from deer, moose, and rabbits over the ground, and voles and mice underground. If you manage the right balance between all of these, the result is rewarding and gratifying and makes you feel alive.

Just like raising kids!

Root Cellar

As we were trying to figure out how to grow endive, we read in the paper that a farm in Danville was offering a seminar on how to create your own root cellar. I could not make it to the seminar but I called them to see if they had any tips on a forcing facility for endive. The person to whom I spoke said no, but he had heard of a local guy who was starting an endive operation. I smiled because he was talking about me.

Life in the Northeast Kingdom

Biking to Town

"Vermont" in French means "green mount," and the description is apt because it is very hilly. People from the city are often referred to as flatlanders – usually a pejorative term. It's beautiful country, but biking in the area is not easy. Our favorite destination was to bike all the way to Craftsbury and back, about a twelve-mile ride, but we often needed to be picked up because the kids had a hard time biking back up the hill. We also learned to hate the monstrous road grader – the big machine that scrapes the top layer of a dirt road to re-level it. Biking on a road after this machine has passed by is pure torture on the hands – the vibrations are very strong and never end until one gets to the smooth paved roads. So I would take the kids through the dirt roads then to the paved road to town.

At every intersection we saw large black circles of tire marks – donuts made by young drivers at night, spinning their wheels. Every intersection had a set of donuts. It so much reminded me of Lebanon.

The kids would look forward to the ride because the destination was an ice cream cone for a dollar at the village store, which is a gas station and a store at the same time. We would get the ice cream and sit out front on the bench and watch the procession of people ambling into the store buying some small items and strolling back out. We loved our bike rides to town and they were dubbed the "Tour de Craftsbury." We also created the "Tour de Paquette," a smaller loop without the ice cream stop. Guests would find it funny that the kids would come up to me and ask simply can we do the Tour de Craftsbury as if it were a common sporting or tour event.

Fireworks

During one of our day trips to Canada to brush up on our French we stopped in Irasburg, near the Canadian border just off Interstate 91, at a place that sold fireworks. Lamia was not interested but I insisted that she come to the store because I did not want to create the usual cliché image of the boys interested in weapons, fireworks, and anything that blew up, and the girls not interested. But I think it is a genetic thing – girls see no value in things that explode. So we all went into the store, which was a garage converted to a store attached to a house (the owner's, I assumed). The garage had shelves all around and even the middle was packed with fireworks. Not your usual simple firecrackers; these were the real deal. We bought a lot and could not wait to try them out.

My near-death experience started at 8:30 that evening. I took one of the mortar tubes and nailed it to a board (I did this based on the suggestion of the owner – none of the fireworks had any instructions on them). I walked away from the house and placed the board with the tube on the ground. Henry and James insisted they wanted to come. Henry wisely suggested that I should put the ball-shaped explosive in the tube *first*, and *then* light the fuse. I told him, don't worry – I grew up during the war in Lebanon and I can handle fireworks in Vermont.

James, Henry and I were huddled around the tube when I lit the fuse. It started burning much faster than I expected – everyone was talking and the ball suddenly fell out of my hand. I panicked because any moment it could explode on the ground. I yelled for the kids to get back and I grabbed the ball with the fuse burning my hand and threw it into the tube exactly one second before it blew up and soared up into the air. I barely had time to move my head from above the tube. The side of my hair was singed and I really felt bad – this could have been very dangerous for the kids and me.

The same day I saw our neighbor who had just gotten back from his family's Fourth of July celebration. He told me that they had a lot of fireworks and decided to use an old mortar tube that was already nailed to a board. The tube was not strong enough and the mortar exploded on the ground and lit all the other fireworks they had ready for show. Everyone ran in every direction. I laughed and felt a bit better.

The Bugle

During a visit to the town of Barton – a really cute town – we stopped at an antiques store and everyone was allowed to buy one thing with the money they had earned helping compost and seed the vegetable garden. This was a great moment; instead of kids buying a piece of junk made in China, each had full range to buy any reasonably priced item from this antiques-and-junk store. James bought an old ukulele for $4 that had only two strings, Leslie bought a small wooden trinket box with some jewelry for $5, and Henry bought a metal car from the nineteen-fifties. Lamia found a small upholstered stool that would be perfect in the living room, and I unearthed a vintage army bugle from the 1800s.

Lamia took her stool to Paul the upholsterer to have it reupholstered with a vintage linen flour sack fabric she had found on eBay. Paul was an Englishman who had moved to the area a while back and we had met him after reading an article on him in the local paper. He was a really nice guy, and during every visit to his place along with a discussion about upholstering there was also a discussion about vegetable gardening. He was an avid gardener and Lamia loved talking to him about plants and vegetables. After one of the visits to Paul, Lamia came back exclaiming, "How could we have forgotten to plant potatoes?" Paul had given her some wonderful Russian fingerling potatoes from his garden and after having them for dinner that night, we vowed never to forget to plant potatoes again.

I brought my bugle back home and behaved like a kid after Christmas. I quickly went online and found YouTube movies showing people playing the bugle (now you know that I figure out how to do most things from watching YouTube). My goal was to learn how to play "Reveille," which means "wake up" in French, and was the tune bugle players in the army used to wake up the troops. I practiced every day for at least half an hour until one day I had mastered the tune. From then on every time we had guests, based on how I felt about their need to sleep I would sound the bugle at 6:00 am, sometimes 7:00, and for guests who really helped out around the farm sometimes as late as 8:00 am.

Lamia complained that we had come to Vermont for peace and quiet, not bugle calls.

Unplugged

When we bought the farm we learned that the immediate neighborhood did not have cell phone coverage, but the Edgertons had signed up for a wireless Internet connection that we kept. We decided that we would not have a TV. The landline always has a permanent hum, probably due to the distance from the house to the main office, and often times just goes dead. We found that up the road there was a spot that had cell reception, and a lot of people drive their cars and park there to make calls on their cells. There is also another place next to the tree on the side of the driveway where my cell phone was able to receive text messages and emails but no phone calls. Once I was walking by that tree and the phone started vibrating.

The kids spent some time getting used to not having a TV. They found some loopholes in the system and used the Internet to watch kids' movies. We quickly caught on to that and banned the Internet unless it was raining outside. The consequence of this authoritarian, ruthless, and heartless ban was a very fast-growing love of reading. Henry once read for eight hours in a single day. We had to force him outside for some fresh air and ban excessive reading, especially when it was an escape from doing chores.

We started to have more conversations. Every night I would tell the kids a long story that sometimes took days to finish. Long-forgotten games such as chess, bridge, Risk, and Monopoly reappeared in our lives. My favorite time was teaching the kids how to play a simplified version of bridge and playing it practically every night.

Hay Season

Hay season is another sacred time in the area. Most people who have fields that are not used for corn or other crops grow hay. They either use it for their own animals or sell it to people who own horses. Hay is cut twice a summer and should be harvested dry. So when the hay is ready and needs to be cut before a rainfall, it is an all-out effort. The hay is baled into large round bales that are then covered in white plastic to protect them from the elements. Headlights of tractors are often seen in the fields at dusk, and as night falls the big white marshmallows gather on the edges of the fields.

Everett Demeritt

We were told that if you drove up Paquette Road and made a left at what they call the "T" and then drove for another minute or two, you'd arrive at the house of Everett Demeritt, one of the old-timers of Craftsbury whose family moved here one hundred years ago. He is a veteran of the Korean War and ran a wood mill on his farm. Everett, we were told, was in his eighties, and we learned a lot about him and his family because The Hardwick *Gazette* ran a story on the family's centennial anniversary of moving to Craftsbury.

Once at a party at Harry's house I met a man and I asked him how long he had been in the area.

He answered, "Not too long – thirty-seven years."

We were such newcomers compared to Everett and some of the other old-timers! I knew that if we were in the local army, our rank would be no more than a foot soldier.

One day Lamia was weeding in the perennial beds when a pickup pulled up in the driveway. Everyone had a pickup truck and everyone came by to say hello and to check us out. The elderly man behind the wheel was not a familiar face so Lamia said hello.

"And who might you be, young lady?" he said.

At first Lamia was a bit surprised and wanted to say, "This is my house and my driveway, who might you be?" but she checked that impulse and introduced herself instead.

At this point the crotchety old man warmed up a bit and introduced himself: "My name is Everett Demeritt and I heard that you bought the Edgerton's house and I wanted to say hello."

I quickly joined the conversation because I was not about to miss out on a conversation with Everett Demeritt – it promised to be really interesting. We talked for an hour about the area and the town, and about how his family had been here for a hundred years. He told us that we had an excellent scarf joint in the house.

He knew woodwork, and indeed on the first floor two large supporting beams were joined together – probably when the house was built in 1865 – by a scarf joint. Everett also told us with great pride that on the upcoming Fourth of July he was going to walk in the parade with his son and grandson – all veterans or currently in the military. We told him that he must be very proud and it made us think about how few people in and around our circle of friends and acquaintances were in the military. His grandson was being called to Afghanistan.

Burning the Brush Pile

In all the weeding, dividing and pruning we had performed throughout the spring, summer and fall, we had accumulated a lot of brush in the field below the pond. One day, when all the necessary variables were in place I said to the kids, "It's time to burn it!"

I was advised to do it either during or right after a rainy day, as this would keep the fire under control. I took matches and cardboard and went with Henry and James. After trying to ignite the brush and burning all the paper and cardboard, I had no fire. Starting a brush pile was harder then I thought! It was late so we postponed the burning until the next day.

The following day I came back with more paper and cardboard and some gasoline. I poured gas all around the pile the asked the kids to back up a bit and I lit the fire.

The gas did not burn – it exploded. Even Lamia, who was reading with Leslie in the house, felt the explosion. Clearly gasoline was not the right answer.

The third day I came back with fire starters from the wood stove and it was a success. We had a huge bonfire that lasted all night. We all gathered around the fire, watched the sparks fly high up into the air, felt warmed by its heat while our backs froze. The children had a blast throwing pine cuttings into the fire and watching them sizzle like fireworks. We told stories; we tested our courage by seeing who could go the furthest into the darkness before having to turn back; we sat quietly and watched our bonfire burn. I cannot think of a more wonderful way to spend an evening with one's family. Every one of us has a fleece from that night with small burn holes caused by the many sparks that rained on us that evening.

Phone Numbers

In the Northeast Kingdom, if you ask anyone for a phone number they just give you the last four digits. They assume that you know the three-digit exchange for the town. In our neighborhood it's 586 for Craftsbury, 472 for Hardwick, and 888 for Morrisville. It reminded me of my village in Lebanon where everyone already knew the local exchange numbers.

From the Northeast Kingdom to Senegal

Harry came over one day wearing a funky hat – it was definitely not a local design and it reminded me of a hat I had seen somewhere. He asked me to try and guess but I couldn't pinpoint the design or ethnic origin.

It was a Pashtun hat from Afghanistan and Pakistan, and Harry laughingly said that he was going to wear it during his trip to Senegal. He was flying to Senegal to his see his daughter who was spending a year abroad. This was impressive – from Craftsbury to Senegal! I complimented him on his desire to push his kids to travel the world before settling in. If they were to come back to Craftsbury it would be by choice, not from necessity or lack of options. Harry was going to wear the same hat to the Obama inauguration. He drove all the way from Vermont to Washington, D.C. with his son Jackson to participate in the inauguration.

Canoe

I decided that we needed a canoe to use on the pond and the lakes in the area. The region's various lakes are magnificent – Crystal Lake, Caspian Lake, and the one really close by, Green River Reservoir, which is just a ten-minute car ride from the farm. I looked on Craigslist and found a guy in Newton selling his Old Town canoe with everything – paddles, a small electric engine, life vests, and ropes. We drove our Volvo with the kids to his house and paid him for the canoe and I asked him why he was selling it. He replied that he was moving into kayaks.

We loaded the huge and extremely heavy wooden canoe on the roof of the car and tied it to the best of our ability. We set off for Vermont and it was a scary drive. Lamia decided that she was not driving all the way to Vermont with this thing, so we changed our plans and had it shipped with some other items.

The canoe was so heavy that we rarely used

it. We once took it fishing to the reservoir and twice it fell on Lamia's feet, and getting it on the roof of the car was a challenge.

Our fishing experience in the boat was not much of a success. We bought some worms from the gas station in Morrisville, and a fishing pole from a local store. But no one wanted to touch the squirming worms, much less put them on the hook. They spent the rest of their lives in the refrigerator.

One day if we buy a pickup truck we might use the canoe more often. I now understand why the guy was selling the canoe for kayaks – they are much easier to use and transport.

Traveling Salespeople

One day yet another ubiquitous black pickup truck stopped in front of the house. I walked up to the driver and greeted him. The man was wearing a Polo shirt with the logo of a company on it and next to him was another guy with a similar shirt.

With a very thick southern accent the man said, "How are you doing today? Are you a farmer? Is this a farm?"

Not sure how to answer I said, "Why do you ask?"

"Well, sir, we're selling equipment at a discount."

He came out of his truck and opened the tailgate and showed me three machines – an electric generator, a pressure washer, and a compressor, all still in their plastic wrap. He said that these had a value of ten thousand dollars but I could have them for two thousand. They were polite but aggressive sales people and they both worked the deal hard.

I immediately thought that they were selling stolen goods. The minute they sensed my reluctance they said, "Thank you very much for your time," and drove away.

Later I asked around and these two guys were seen everywhere, and in fact had brought a container of equipment and were selling it door-to-door. From what I hear it was legitimate. Eventually I got used to people dropping by to try to sell their goods or services.

House Numbers

Our house number is 791, and on either side our neighbors are at least half a mile away. This was perplexing – why was the number so specific? Was someone keeping the numbers spread apart for future construction or development? Also, the names of the roads were interesting – some were the last names of the owners and some were random names.

I asked around and found the reasons. The house numbers are the distance from the main road, and we were 0.791 miles from the asphalt road called Wild Branch. And fifteen years ago the state decided to give names to all the dirt roads and asked people to decide and agree on a name or be assigned one. We drove past a road in the area called Old Fart Road. I don't know whether it was assigned as retribution or chosen by the people living on the road. Maybe it was a comic variation of Old Farm Road, of which there are dozens in Vermont. The main purpose for all of this street naming was to help the fire department find their destination.

Circus Smirkus

All of the general stores in the area, like the Village Store, the General Store, and The Willey's store, operate by the principle of "If we don't have it – you don't need it." Greensboro, the next town over, has a more affluent summer lakeside population with a very old tradition of summer folk coming to the area. The stores all have bulletin boards outside with all kinds of events and fliers on them. That is how we found our cleaning ladies (a team of exceptional young ladies who are teachers by day) and our horseback riding instructor, Jennifer.

We also discovered Circus Smirkus. Many years ago Rob Mermin, a young man of seventeen, left his parents to join the circus. He eventually came home, and in 1987 in an old farmhouse in Greensboro he created his own circus where all the performers were kids. Their first tour lasted one week around Vermont, but now they tour around the world and have a circus school. At the end of each season they put together a show with multiple performances ending with the final week in their home town of Greensboro.

Of course we had to go! The Circus Smirkus tent was set up in a field outside of Greensboro, with Port-o-Lets outside and another tent for snacks and souvenirs. The show was not high-tech but so passionate and heartwarming that we had tears at the end of each performance we attended. The tent was packed and the creativity and sensitivity of the different skits was very touching. Circus Smirkus became a yearly stop on our calendar and a must-see family event.

Antiques and Uniques

For one day each year the town of Craftsbury opens its town commons to antique dealers of all kinds, and people flock from all parts of the state to walk around and find hidden treasures. We always walk around the tents looking for things of interest. The first year we found a lady who was selling signs painted on wood with a finish that looked like aged metal. The signs were meant for the outdoors so I asked her if she could custom-make a sign and she said sure. I wrote down "Rocambole" and picked a style and gave her my phone number to call when the sign was ready. Four weeks later we picked it up in Hardwick and hung it on the side of the shed.

The following year during our visit to the show a man from Saint Johnsbury was selling very nice and very sturdy cutting boards made out of maple, birch, or cherry. One of the boards had a checkered pattern and it gave me the idea – yet again – to ask if he could do a custom design.

Four weeks later I had my new chessboard, two inches thick with sixty-four two-inch-wide squares. The chessboard sits in the living room as an art piece as well as game.

We take a lot of pride in patronizing local artists and businesses. Lamia ordered a butter holder from a local pottery maker in Craftsbury. The butter dish was the old-fashioned way one should keep butter. The dish has two parts – a cup that holds water and ice and a smaller round cup where the butter goes. You pack the butter into the smaller cup and when not being used the butter cup is flipped and placed upside down over the water cup. The water seals in the freshness. The dish is left outside of the fridge and the butter is always soft.

Buses Are Welcome

From Interstate 91, the drive north to Craftsbury goes through the town of Danville on Route 2 west, then turns north on Route 15 to Hardwick. Where Routes 2 and 15 intersect is a rest area with a couple of general stores and a large parking area with a sign that says, "Buses are welcome." Passing this section especially at the beginning when we were not used to the road was a sign that we were on the right track. I arbitrarily decided that for good luck every person in the car had to say, "Buses are welcome." At first I met with resistance but I insisted that it would be bad luck if we didn't say it. The family went with the flow and the silly idea became a tradition. To this day we have never passed this area without saying, "Buses are welcome," even when the kids are sleeping or about to sleep they can either say it early or if they forget Lamia and I would say it on their behalf. This family tradition created out of thin air will forever remain a childhood memory for our kids. In a world focused on material goods and material legacies, giving our kids memories has the most value.

Farm Stands

Every Saturday we went to the supermarket to buy groceries, including cheese and other items – that is, until we discovered the terrific farm stands in the area. The two we visit the most are Peets, which is in town, and Robert Link, right down the dirt road from our house. You pay based on the honor system – you take what you want, weigh it if need be, and leave the money in a drawer.

The items change all the time based on the season and availability. Once Lamia brought home a jar of honey she had bought from Robert Link's stand. Robert's father kept bees and this was his honey that he packed into old pasta sauce jars. This was the best honey I had ever had, and to add to the romance, the honey gave me a warm, homey feeling. I started to wonder why it felt so good. I ran to the computer and searched for honeybees and how far they go from the hive to get pollen. The answer is that they go up to four miles. Robert's stand is a mile and a half from our house. His bees were almost certainly coming to our land and taking the pollen from our wildflowers and also perhaps from the perennial beds. I had no way of proving that some of our pollen was used, but I liked the idea.

The Local Food

There are two ways to cook. One is to choose a recipe or plan a meal, and then acquire the products and ingredients for the preparation. The other is the opposite – find what is available, fresh, and inspiring, and then create a meal. Needless to say, living at Rocambole has inspired us to follow the second path, and what a better place than Vermont and the farmstands of the area to find inspiration for the creation of great meals.

Once we began to use local foods like fresh eggs, fresh milk, organic grass-fed meat, and pasture-raised organic chicken, cooking became a delight. We came to see gastronomy through the local organic lens, and our approach to eating was transformed.

Our new appreciation of gastronomy started at breakfast with local farm-fresh eggs, either scrambled or used in crêpes. At home in Boston I had often made crêpes, but at breakfast in Vermont the amazed kids asked why they were so good. I replied that it was the eggs – the ones from the supermarket just don't taste as good. With some maple syrup sprinkled on top you have what I call one of the small pleasures of life – *les petits plaisirs de la vie*. Blueberries are optional but no one ever opted out. Breakfast was washed down with local apple cider and the day was off to a good start.

The goal is to have everything served at the table come from within ten miles of the house, and the closer the better. And we often succeed; at many meals the only items that are not local are salt, pepper, olive oil, and ketchup.

Lunch might be a sandwich using local bread with local cheese from Bonnieview Farm in Craftsbury with some lettuce, basil, and tomato from the garden.

Dinner is often a pork chop from Applecheek Farm in Hyde Park with a cream, pepper, and mustard sauce, served with green peppers and potato sticks and a side salad – all local. Stepping out of the kitchen to cut some homegrown basil or coriander adds to the pleasure.

Once we cooked a delicious chicken in the oven and we realized that we had cooked it upside down. It was because the chicken breast was not as large as what we were used to. We learned that a normal chicken should not have a huge breast, which is often a sign of hormones or other unnatural additives. The free-range chicken had so much taste that an oven-roasted chicken with root vegetables all around it has become our favorite Sunday lunch.

Because they are always eaten before the meal is ready, the items that never make it to the table are the cherry tomatoes from Pete's Greens. If they are anywhere in the kitchen they are eaten like candy. Once I hid some so I could enjoy them later, but my plan was quickly discovered and the tomatoes disappeared.

Lunch with Friends

To celebrate the end of the project, on a nice Sunday in July 2010 we invited to lunch everyone who had worked on the house and the land. I knew that the evolution of the house and land would never end, but this was to thank everyone for their work and care during the first few years of our stewardship of the property. At that moment I realized that the workers, builders and contractors had all transformed to neighbors and friends, and we felt blessed to be welcomed in the community.

Thank You and Acknowledgments

I would like to conclude this book by thanking all the people who helped us refocus our life and understand what really matters. I realized that I have so much more to learn. It is always assumed that the old teach the young, the successful teach the less successful, the able teach the disabled, and the educated teach the uneducated. We go to seminars to listen to successful businesspeople and we are inundated with interviews with the infamous and the notorious.

The real lesson is that often it is the opposite. We never hear about the housewife and mother who spends her time raising her kids without fame, prestige, or media attention.

Before getting married I went on a three-week Outward Bound camping trip and one of the planned challenges was to climb a fourteen-thousand-foot peak – at midnight! I was young and fit and wanted to get to the top first. One of the guides was a blacksmith by trade, as well as a mountain guide and Outward Bound director. He took me aside and said, "Don't climb straight to the peak and miss the point. The story is on the side of the mountain. You're going to spend six hours going up and down and only ten to fifteen minutes at the top."

I set a goal for myself to write this book before I turned forty years old on November 28, 2010. If you are reading this sentence it means that I did it!

Ziad

Made in the USA
Charleston, SC
11 February 2011